Policies and Practices to Minimize Police Use of Force Internationally

Committee on Evidence to Advance Reform in the
Global Security and Justice Sectors

Committee on Law and Justice

Division of Behavioral and Social Sciences and Education

A Consensus Study Report of

The National Academies of
SCIENCES • ENGINEERING • MEDICINE

THE NATIONAL ACADEMIES PRESS
Washington, DC
www.nap.edu

THE NATIONAL ACADEMIES PRESS   500 Fifth Street, NW   Washington, DC 20001

This activity was supported by contracts between the National Academy of Sciences and the Bureau of International Narcotics and Law Enforcement Affairs of the U.S. Department of State, Award No. SINLEC20CA3213. Any opinions, findings, conclusions, or recommendations expressed in this publication do not necessarily reflect the views of any organization or agency that provided support for the project.

International Standard Book Number-13: 978-0-309-68910-6
International Standard Book Number-10: 0-309-68910-4
Digital Object Identifier: https://doi.org/10.17226/26582

Additional copies of this publication are available from the National Academies Press, 500 Fifth Street, NW, Keck 360, Washington, DC 20001; (800) 624-6242 or (202) 334-3313; http://www.nap.edu.

Copyright 2022 by the National Academy of Sciences. All rights reserved.

Printed in the United States of America

Suggested citation: National Academies of Sciences, Engineering, and Medicine. 2022. *Policies and Practices to Minimize Police Use of Force Internationally.* Washington, DC: The National Academies Press. https://doi.org/10.17226/26582.

The National Academies of
SCIENCES · ENGINEERING · MEDICINE

The **National Academy of Sciences** was established in 1863 by an Act of Congress, signed by President Lincoln, as a private, nongovernmental institution to advise the nation on issues related to science and technology. Members are elected by their peers for outstanding contributions to research. Dr. Marcia McNutt is president.

The **National Academy of Engineering** was established in 1964 under the charter of the National Academy of Sciences to bring the practices of engineering to advising the nation. Members are elected by their peers for extraordinary contributions to engineering. Dr. John L. Anderson is president.

The **National Academy of Medicine** (formerly the Institute of Medicine) was established in 1970 under the charter of the National Academy of Sciences to advise the nation on medical and health issues. Members are elected by their peers for distinguished contributions to medicine and health. Dr. Victor J. Dzau is president.

The three Academies work together as the **National Academies of Sciences, Engineering, and Medicine** to provide independent, objective analysis and advice to the nation and conduct other activities to solve complex problems and inform public policy decisions. The National Academies also encourage education and research, recognize outstanding contributions to knowledge, and increase public understanding in matters of science, engineering, and medicine.

Learn more about the National Academies of Sciences, Engineering, and Medicine at **www.nationalacademies.org**.

The National Academies of
SCIENCES • ENGINEERING • MEDICINE

Consensus Study Reports published by the National Academies of Sciences, Engineering, and Medicine document the evidence-based consensus on the study's statement of task by an authoring committee of experts. Reports typically include findings, conclusions, and recommendations based on information gathered by the committee and the committee's deliberations. Each report has been subjected to a rigorous and independent peer-review process and it represents the position of the National Academies on the statement of task.

Proceedings published by the National Academies of Sciences, Engineering, and Medicine chronicle the presentations and discussions at a workshop, symposium, or other event convened by the National Academies. The statements and opinions contained in proceedings are those of the participants and are not endorsed by other participants, the planning committee, or the National Academies.

For information about other products and activities of the National Academies, please visit www.nationalacademies.org/about/whatwedo.

**COMMITTEE ON EVIDENCE TO ADVANCE REFORM IN
THE GLOBAL SECURITY AND JUSTICE SECTORS**

LAWRENCE W. SHERMAN (*Chair*), University of Cambridge Institute of Criminology
BEATRIZ ABIZANDA, Inter-American Development Bank
YANILDA MARÍA GONZÁLEZ, Kennedy School of Government, Harvard University
GUY GROSSMAN, University of Pennsylvania
JOHN L. HAGAN, Northwestern University
KAREN HALL, Rule of Law Collaborative, University of South Carolina
CYNTHIA LUM, George Mason University
EMILY OWENS, University of California, Irvine
JUSTICE TANKEBE, University of Cambridge Institute of Criminology

JULIE ANNE SCHUCK, *Study Director*
SARAH PERUMATTAM, *Senior Program Assistant (until October 2021)*
SUNIA YOUNG, *Senior Program Assistant (from October 2021)*
ABIGAIL ALLEN, *Associate Program Officer (from November 2021)*
EMILY P. BACKES, *Deputy Director, Committee on Law and Justice*
MEGAN SNAIR, *Technical Writer*

COMMITTEE ON LAW AND JUSTICE

ROBERT D. CRUTCHFIELD (*Chair*), University of Washington (*retired*)
SALLY S. SIMPSON (*Vice Chair*), University of Maryland
ROD K. BRUNSON, Northeastern University
SHAWN D. BUSHWAY, University at Albany
PREETI CHAUHAN, John Jay College of Criminal Justice
KIMBERLÉ W. CRENSHAW, University of California, Los Angeles
MARK S. JOHNSON, Howard University
CYNTHIA LUM, George Mason University
JOHN M. MACDONALD, University of Pennsylvania
KAREN J. MATHIS, American Bar Association (*retired*), University of Denver
THEODORE A. MCKEE, United States Court of Appeals for the Third Circuit
SAMUEL L. MYERS JR., University of Minnesota
EMILY OWENS, University of California, Irvine
CYNTHIA RUDIN, Duke University
WILLIAM J. SABOL, Georgia State University
LINDA A. TEPLIN, Northwestern University Medical School

NATACHA BLAIN, *Director*
EMILY P. BACKES, *Associate Director*

Acknowledgments

This report would not have been possible without the contributions of many people. First, we thank the sponsor of this study, the U.S. Department of State, Bureau of International Narcotics and Law Enforcement Affairs, for requesting and supporting this endeavor. We have admired the sponsor's dedication to an evidence-led approach to further its programming.

Special thanks go to the members of the study committee, who dedicated extensive time, thought, and energy to this report. In addition to its own research and deliberations, the committee received input from several outside sources, whose willingness to share their perspectives and experience was essential to the committee's work. We thank Mark Berlin (Marquette University), Derryck Martin Espinoza (Trinidad & Tobago Police Service), Claudia Flores (University of Chicago), Sanja Kutnjak Ivkovich (Michigan State University), Sean Tait (African Policing Civilian Oversight Forum), and Stephen Williams (University of the West Indies). The committee also gathered information through two commissioned papers. We thank Ignacio Cano (State University of Rio de Janeiro) and Geoffrey Alpert (University of South Carolina) and colleagues, Kyle McLean (Clemson University) and Seth Stoughton (University of South Carolina) for their papers and for contributing both to the discussion at the committee's information gathering workshop and to findings in the report.

The committee also wishes to extend its gratitude to the staff of the National Academies of Sciences, Engineering, and Medicine, in particular to: study director Julie Schuck, who made critical substantive contributions to the conception, writing, and editing of the report; Jessalyn Brogan Walker who was the study director through June 2021, identified and prepared commissioned paper authors as well as assembled suggestions of experts for the committee's workshop; Emily Backes who provided substantive writing and editing contributions and critical oversight and direction for the project; Abigail Allen who played an essential role in providing thorough and rigorous research and writing for the project; as well as both Sarah Perumattam and Sunia Young who provided key administrative and logistical support while making sure the committee process ran efficiently and smoothly. Further, we want to extend thanks to the National Academies Research Center, particularly Anne Marie Houppert and Rebecca Morgan, provided valuable research assistance. From the Division of Behavioral and Social Sciences and Education, we thank Kirsten Sampson-Snyder, who shepherded the report through the review process, and Douglas Sprunger, who assisted with the report's communication and dissemination. We also thank technical writer Megan Snair for quickly summarizing the presentations and discussions from the committee's workshop and, with editor Marc DeFrancis, provided skillful writing and editing of the report manuscript.

This Consensus Study Report was reviewed in draft form by individuals chosen for their diverse perspectives and technical expertise. The purpose of this independent review is to provide candid and critical comments that will assist the National Academies of Sciences, Engineering, and Medicine in making each published report as sound as possible and to ensure that it meets the institutional standards for quality, objectivity, evidence, and responsiveness to the study charge. The review comments and draft manuscript remain confidential to protect the integrity of the deliberative process.

We thank the following individuals for their review of this report: Cynthia M. Beall, Department of Anthropology, Case Western Reserve University; Felipe M. Goncalves, Department of Economics, University of California, Los Angeles; Ross Hendy, School of Social Sciences, Monash University, Australia; Edward Maguire, School of Criminology and Criminal Justice, Arizona State University; Louise Porter, School of Criminology and Criminal Justice, Griffith University; Gregory K. Ridgway, Department of Criminology, University of Pennsylvania; Nazli Yildirim Schierkolk, Independent Expert on Police Accountability, Europe; and Lucía Tiscornia, Center for Research and Teaching in Economics, Division of International Studies, Centro de Investigación y Docencia Económicas, Mexico City.

Although the reviewers listed above provided many constructive comments and suggestions, they were not asked to endorse the conclusions or recommendations of this report nor did they see the final draft before its release. The review of this report was overseen by Alex R. Piquero, Department of Sociology and Criminology, University of Miami, and Philip J. Cook, Sanford School of Public Policy, Duke University. They were responsible for making certain that an independent examination of this report was carried out in accordance with the standards of the National Academies and that all review comments were carefully considered. Responsibility for the final content rests entirely with the authoring committee and the National Academies.

Contents

SUMMARY   1

1 INTRODUCTION   5
   The Committee's Charge, 6
   Approach to the Study, 8
   Scope of the Problem, 10
   Levels of Analysis and Causes of Excessive Force, 12
   Societal Attitudes Toward Police Violence, 13
   Organization of the Report, 14

2 PRACTICES DESIGNED TO REGULATE AND CONTROL
   USE OF FORCE   15
   Laws and Standards, 16
   External Oversight Bodies, 23
   Police Training and Evaluations, 26
   Barriers to Internal Control Mechanisms, 31
   Technological Innovations, 34
   Administrative Incentives, 37
   Conclusion, 39

3 COMMITTEE'S CONCLUSIONS AND RECOMMENDATIONS   41
   Data Needs, 42
   Use of Force Policies, 46
   Training for Police Officers, 47
   Oversight and Supervision, 49

REFERENCES 51

Appendix   Biographical Sketches of Committee Members and Staff   61

Summary

Injury and death from use of excessive force by police officers remain a common concern in countries across the globe. Despite local, national, and international attempts to legislate and provide guidance for police use of force, there continue to be global accounts of excessive force by law enforcement. Reports of officer-involved killings, injuries to citizens, attempts to control protests as well as demonstrations with chemical irritants, rubber bullets, and sometimes shooting into crowds with live ammunition frequently appear in the press worldwide. However, reliable data on and accounting for these incidents are both lacking.

A large network of international and regional organizations, bilateral donors, international financial institutions, and civil society organizations aims to work with governments to improve policing practices and reduce police use of excessive force. As a part of that network, the U.S. Department of State, through its Bureau of International Narcotics and Law Enforcement Affairs (INL), provides foreign assistance to and supports capacity building for criminal justice systems and police organizations in approximately 90 countries. Like many donors, it strives to direct its resources to the most effective approaches to achieve its mission.

As part of its efforts to distill available knowledge and improve its programs, INL asked the Committee on Law and Justice of the National Academies of Sciences, Engineering, and Medicine to convene an ad hoc committee to review, assess, and reach consensus on existing evidence on policing institutions, police practices and capacities, and police legitimacy in the international context. A committee was assembled with expertise in criminology, economics, international and organized crime, law, policing, and political science. The committee was tasked to produce five reports, addressing questions of interest to INL and the State Department. This report, the third in this series, is in response to the following questions: *What policies and practices for police use of force are effective in promoting the rule of law and protecting the population (including officers themselves)? What is known about effective practices for implementing those policies and practices in recruitment, training, and internal affairs?*

Police use of force is an expansive topic with numerous scientific questions yet to be studied and answered. The studies that have been done examine policies, training, selection of officers, supervision, and accountability in some contexts; however, many of the policies and programs implemented by police agencies have yet to be rigorously evaluated. In addition, deficiencies in reliable records on police use of force impedes progress in evaluating the effectiveness of interventions. Most evidence, when it does exist, concerns incidents of lethal force, since deaths are more likely to be reported than other harms. However, even this information can be unreliable in some countries.

While the existing knowledge base is limited, research in this area is growing. The determination of policies and practices to minimize excessive force by police cannot be made on robust evidence at this time. Still, there are sound theoretical assumptions and reliable findings across policing studies to inform promising approaches and efforts to advance knowledge in the area. This report, drawing on the committee's understanding of the scientific literature on police use of force and normative positions to promote the rule of law and protect the population, offers the committee's consensus view of promising actions to be taken by international donors in their efforts to strengthen the effectiveness of law enforcement agencies. The committee's recommendations are presented here and discussed further in Chapter 3.

RECOMMENDATION 1: Significant gaps in measurement related to police use of force exist. International donor organizations, such as the U.S. Department of State, Bureau of International Narcotics and Law Enforcement Affairs, should support local and/or national systems in the collection and dissemination of standardized information about use of force by law enforcement officers. Priority should be given to the documentation and publication by an independent medical examiner or coroner of every case where someone (citizen or police) dies as a result of a police encounter. Where these systems do not function reliably, donors should strongly support their creation or efforts to improve them.

RECOMMENDATION 2: While most use of force by police is not lethal, frequent incidences of excessive force can cause great harm to the public as it can undermine the rule of law, trust in the police, and in state institutions more broadly. International donor organizations such as U.S. Department of State, Bureau of International Narcotics and Law Enforcement Affairs should encourage as well as fund police agencies to develop and enforce digital record-keeping on each use of force incident with or with potential of serious injuries, such as all police-citizen interactions where firearms or other weapons are employed. These records should identify officers using force, the nature of force, the weapon used, the locations of the incidents, the time and date of each incident, as well as personal identifiers and demographic information for citizens involved. Technical assistance should be granted to develop ongoing analyses of the patterns of less-than-lethal force incidents, including concentrations of events among individual officers, specific places, and times.

RECOMMENDATION 3: Innovations intended to minimize police use of force should be supported by international donor organizations, such as U.S. Department of State, Bureau of International Narcotics and Law Enforcement Affairs. Police agencies should work in partnerships with independent social and data scientists to design impact assessments in order to evaluate and continuously improve their reform programs.

RECOMMENDATION 4: International donor organizations, such as U.S. Department of State, Bureau of International Narcotics and Law Enforcement Affairs, should work with implementing partners to ensure that policies on police use of force have been developed or reviewed in consultation with relevant police oversight bodies and ombuds institutions. These policies should be impartially enforced, clearly defined, aligned with human rights standards, inclusive of mechanisms for civilian oversight, communicated to police officers through ongoing training opportunities, and regularly reviewed for effectiveness.

RECOMMENDATION 5: International donor organizations should incentivize robust evaluations of training outcomes through extra funding assistance for partners willing to evaluate training programs, particularly any programs aimed at improving officers' skills at de-escalating situations before resorting to use of force. Where possible, evaluations should be done by comparing on-the-job actions taken by training participants and non-participants and linking completion of these programs with official records and data on use of force over time.

1

Introduction

Internationally, many governments, citizens, and police themselves are troubled by continued uses of force that occur too frequently, are avoidable, seem excessive, or are perceived to disproportionately target specific populations. The reaction to the death of George Floyd in an encounter with police in the United States is just one example that gave rise to worldwide demonstrations, even amid a global pandemic. While police officers globally are authorized to use physical force in certain situations, for example, as a means of self-defense or to protect others from an attack, excessive use of physical force is one of the most prevalent forms of police misconduct (U.S. Department of State, 2016). National governments and their citizens rely on law enforcement officials to uphold the rule of law (ROL) and protect human life. When police fail to uphold internationally recognized standards regarding the use of force (see Chapter 2), they violate fundamental human rights, including the rights to life, liberty, and security of person, the prohibition of torture or other cruel, inhuman or degrading treatment, and respect for the inherent dignity of the human person (United Nations, 2009).

A large network of international and regional organizations, bilateral donors, international financial institutions, and civil society organizations aims to work with governments to curb and eliminate violations at the hands of police. As a part of that network, the U.S. Department of State, through its Bureau of International Narcotics and Law Enforcement Affairs (INL), provides foreign assistance and supports capacity building for criminal justice systems and police organizations in approximately 90 countries. In 2018, guided by The Foundations for Evidence-Based Policymaking Act, INL created the Office of Knowledge Management to assemble evidence from research to inform its work. To support its efforts to synthesize findings from scientific research, INL asked the Committee on Law and Justice (CLAJ) of the National Academies of Sciences, Engineering, and Medicine (National Academies) to convene an ad hoc consensus committee to review and assess existing evidence on policing institutions, police practices and capacities, and police legitimacy in the international context.

THE COMMITTEE'S CHARGE

The National Academies of Science, Engineering and Medicine assembled the Committee on Evidence to Advance Reform in the Global Security and Justice Sectors ("the committee") to review the available research evidence on how police reform can promote the ROL (including human rights) and protect the public. See Box 1-1 for the committee's perspective on ROL and protection of the population.

The committee comprises experts in criminology, economics, international and organized crime, law, policing, and political science and brings knowledge and experience from a portfolio of work that spans four continents. Such experience includes conducting research and advising governments on police policy in several countries, including but not limited to Afghanistan, Brazil, Colombia, England, Ghana, India, South Korea, Uganda, the United Kingdom, and the United States (see the Appendix for more details).

The committee was charged with producing five reports, each addressing areas of interest to INL (see Box 1-2). To assist with this assignment, the committee developed a series of five public information-gathering sessions to bring together researchers and practitioners with experience in each subtopic to be examined.

This report is the third in this series, addressing the following questions in the committee's charge: **What policies and practices for police use of force are effective in promoting the ROL and protecting the population (including officers themselves)? What is known about effective practices for implementing those policies and practices in recruitment, training, and internal affairs?**[1]

APPROACH TO THE STUDY

Like the others in the series, this report reflects the development of consensus advice to address the questions in the charge. The committee was tasked to carry out the entire study within a year and a half and release

---

[1] Each consensus report in the series of five reports will be released in PDF format in sequence of completion.

> **BOX 1-1**
> **ROL and Protection of the Population**
>
> For the purpose of its study, the committee leverages definitions of the ROL from the United Nations and the U.S. State Department. Neyroud (2021) offers a thorough discussion of the challenges in defining the ROL. Several sources provide succinct definitions of the ROL. For example, the United Nations defines it as:
>
>> A principle of governance in which all persons, institutions, and entities, public and private, including the state itself, are accountable to laws that are publicly promulgated, equally enforced, and independently adjudicated that are consistent with international human rights norms and standards. It requires measures to ensure adherence to the principles of supremacy of law, equality before the law, accountability to the law, fairness in the application of the law, separation of powers, participation in decision-making, legal certainty, avoidance of arbitrariness, and procedural and legal transparency.[a]
>
> The U.S. State Department's Bureau of International Narcotics and Law Enforcement Affairs defines the concept as:
>
>> A principle of governance in which all persons, institutions, and entities, public, and private, including the state itself, are accountable to [domestic] laws that are publicly promulgated, equally enforced, and independently adjudicated, and that are consistent with international human rights norms and standards.[b]
>
> Other dimensions and detailed conditions of the ROL are available in the broad legal and philosophical literature (e.g., Bingham, 2011; O'Donnell, 2004). From a scientific perspective, the committee's primary concern is how any definition of ROL is empirically measured. Given its complexity, ROL is likely to vary in degree both across countries and within them over time. That feature has generated a range of cross-country measures for the ROL (Cheung, 2019; Rajah, 2012; Versteeg and Ginsburg, 2017), each of which tends to observe the kinds of features found in the existing codes of human rights and policing practice promoted by international agencies.
>
> A fundamental component of the ROL is that the state itself be held accountable to the law. As such, the police institution has great responsibility to act in ways consistent with laws and international human rights norms and standards. Adherence to human rights standards, understood as a set of normative commitments (Bottoms and Tankebe, 2017), is related to increased legitimacy in policing, including aspects such as refraining from the abuse of force and providing safety to the citizens to ensure that they can exercise their rights and obligations.
>
> ---
> [a] https://www.un.org/ruleoflaw/what-is-the-rule-of-law/.
> [b] https://www.state.gov/wp-content/uploads/2019/03/222048.pdf.
>
> SOURCE: NASEM, 2021, pp. 18–19.

BOX 1-2
Statement of Task

An ad hoc committee of the National Academies of Sciences, Engineering, and Medicine will consider evidence in the areas of policing institutions, police practices and capacities, and police legitimacy in the international context. The committee will hold a series of five public workshops; each of the workshops will focus on a targeted set of questions of interest to the State Department and serve as the primary data source for a brief consensus report. Drawing on relevant literature, particularly from the international context, the project will inform the State Department's capacity-building activities aimed at strengthening the effectiveness of local, in-country law enforcement agencies, building the technical skills of foreign law enforcement personnel through training and technical assistance, and assisting in institutional police reform at the local level.

Each of the five (5) workshops will bring together experts to discuss the evidence and its implications for the international sector, as well as practitioners using the evidence to implement policy. Some papers may be commissioned for one or more workshops. The committee will issue brief independent consensus reports after each public workshop. These reports will include conclusions and recommendations as appropriate, and provide practical guidance on key implications of the evidence for the field.

1. What organizational policies, structures, or practices (e.g., HR and recruiting, legal authorities, reporting lines, etc.) enable a police service to promote the ROL and protect the population?
2. What are the core knowledge and skills needed for police to promote the ROL and protect the population? What is known about mechanisms (e.g., basic and continuing education or other capacity building programs) for developing the core skills needed for police to promote the ROL and protect the population?
3. **What policies and practices for police use of force are effective in promoting the ROL and protecting the population (including officers themselves)? What is known about effective practices for implementing those policies and practices in recruitment, training, and internal affairs?**
4. What policing practices build community trust and legitimacy in countries with low-to-moderate criminal justice sector capacity?
5. What are the systemic features needed to effectively control high-level corruption, and how can police effectively contribute to efforts to combat high-level corruption?

each of the five reports separately and sequentially during this period. In forming its advice, the committee draws specifically on information from prepared papers and a single workshop on the topic of the third question as well as its years of experience investigating policing policies and practices.

The public workshop entitled *Effective Policies & Practices for Police Use of Force to Promote the Rule of Law and Protect the Population* was held virtually on October 20 and 22, 2021. Workshop participants included members of the committee, representatives from INL, and international researchers and practitioners in the area of policing and use of force. An effort was made to assemble a diverse set of participants who work with or study the police in different contexts, including those in Africa, Latin America, the Middle East, and the United States.

The workshop discussions were framed around commissioned papers prepared by Ignacio Cano, State University of Rio de Janeiro, Brazil, and Geoffrey Alpert, Seth Stoughton, and Kyle McLean, University of South Carolina. Both papers examined existing studies and interventions related to policies and practices that attempt to regulate and control police use of force and provided assessments of the strengths and limitations of the research evidence and data. The Alpert and colleagues (2021) paper reviews available research findings in the areas of policies, training, supervision, selection, and accountability regarding police use of force. The Cano (2021) paper considered policies and measures in six categories: normative approaches in the application of the law, internal control mechanisms, external oversight bodies, training for officers, technology for monitoring, and administrative measures. The committee relied on the assessment and analysis presented in the papers to inform its deliberations.

The workshop provided comparative perspectives on laws and policies for police use of force, the code of silence, the prevalence of torture, and related factors. Presentations also examined the limited and largely disconnected evidence surrounding police use of force and the areas of promise in reducing the use of force in policing. Discussions at the workshop, including those about the commissioned papers, were a primary source of information for the committee's deliberations. It is important to note that while the science of policing, notably the examination of police use of force, has grown in recent years, it is limited in context. Due to the research available and studies presented to the committee, examples in this report tend to favor studies conducted in the United States, United Kingdom, Latin America, and (to a lesser extent) Africa. This does not mean that problems of police misconduct and excessive use of force are limited to these regions, nor does it mean solutions and opportunities are limited to these contexts.

The committee met four times virtually after the workshop to deliberate on what it learned from the papers and heard at the workshop to reach a consensus on conclusions and recommendations for its report. The committee's draft report was subsequently reviewed by a set of similar subject matter experts and revised in response to review in accordance with the National Academies' procedures before being finalized for release.

This report presents the committee's assessment of the information it has gathered and provides guidance to international donors on steps to advance data collection and knowledge building on police use of force incidents and interventions. It focuses on what is known about efforts to reduce the use of excessive force and what aspects of the problem require further research. It does not contain the complete proceedings of the workshop, but instead draws on resources and descriptions from the workshop discussion as relevant.[2]

As a project commissioned to conduct five workshops and produce five reports in a rapid production process, the committee's methods differ somewhat from the single consensus report model, such as the report recently prepared by the ad hoc consensus committee on proactive policing (see NASEM, 2018). The breadth of the current assignment and the speed with which it was required led the committee to rely more on its pre-existing knowledge of the research findings than on systematic reviewing of all available studies—even as new research was published while the project was under way.

SCOPE OF THE PROBLEM

Police use of excessive force is a recognized problem, but the scale is widely debated, in part due to data limitations. There are media reports of injuries and deaths at the hands of law enforcement in nearly every country. In the United States, attention to police misconduct has focused on the killing of unarmed Black men and women (Tate et al., 2022); in Iran, reports capture fatal shootings of protestors by police; and in the Philippines, poor people merely suspected of using or selling drugs are at risk of being shot by police (Amnesty International, 2020a; 2020b). The official numbers from Rio de Janeiro, Brazil, for 2019 put the number of individuals killed by police at 1,810, an average of five per day and a record number since official records began in 1998 (BBC, 2020b). In 2017, military and police personnel from the Russian Republic of Chechnya used excessive force repeatedly in attacks against individuals suspected to be members of the LGBTQ+ community (Benedek, 2018). In Hong Kong, police were accused of responding to peaceful anti-government protests with paramilitary-style

---

[2]Full recordings of the workshop are available at: https://www.nationalacademies.org/event/08-26-2021/evidence-to-advance-reform-in-the-global-security-and-justice-sectors-workshop-3-public-session-1 and https://www.nationalacademies.org/event/08-27-2021/evidence-to-advance-reform-in-the-global-security-and-justice-sectors-workshop-3-public-session-2.

interventions, resulting in a wider pro-democracy movement demanding an investigation into police misconduct (BBC, 2020a; Stott et al., 2020).

In sum, this is an issue recognized by large portions of the public as a problem, even while the extent and nature of the problem might remain unclear. The lack of scientific evidence on the prevalence or correlates of police use of force is directly related to the reluctance of many governments, including the United States, to collect and provide regular data on the number of people killed or wounded during police encounters. Some high-income countries routinely report some of these data (Zimring, 2017), including Australia, Denmark, Germany, Sweden, and the United Kingdom. Yet these are the exceptions. The lack of transparency about the extent of excessive force may pose a major threat to the ROL and to trust in state institutions. In some countries, media and civil society organizations have begun compiling individual cases and generating estimates of people killed in police encounters. These non-governmental efforts to assemble reliable information are encouraging; however, data on police use of force remain limited in most developing countries (Amnesty International, 2021; Cano, 2021; Lethal Force Monitor, 2020; Peeples, 2020; U.S. Commission on Civil Rights, 2018).

Further complicating the problem of estimating the scale of police use of force is ambiguity with respect to the definition of force itself (National Institute of Justice, 2020). Use of force has been defined and interpreted in several ways, including: mere police presence, verbal commands, physical use of force (e.g., defensive restraints, punches, kicks, throws), the use of less-lethal devices (e.g., batons, pepper spray, electro-muscular disruption devices, beanbag rounds), the employment of canines on people, and the use of firearms or other deadly weapons on civilians. Another factor complicating the estimation of the scale of police use of force is the different settings in which use of force takes place, such as during arrests, in custodial settings, or during protests or demonstrations. In the absence of reliable systems for transparency and collection of complaints, data on uses of force in custodial settings can be particularly difficult to document.

How use of force is defined influences how it is measured. Due to the variability in its definition, it is challenging to standardize data collection on use of force across police agencies and countries. For example, limiting the form of "injury" to only fatal outcomes specifically due to the use of firearms can help delineate a common denominator for measurement, given the lack of measurement of other indicators. However, excluding the numerous other instances where use of force occurs, but does not result in death by firearm, leads to an incomplete picture of the occurrences themselves and their adverse consequences, as well as the fatality risk associated with using different kinds of implements (e.g., batons, canines, water cannons).

For the purposes of this report and guidance to international donors, the committee does not attempt to define excessive or reasonable force for all countries at all times. It takes the position that donors should strongly encourage their partner nations to define what excessive force means in their jurisdictions, improve their transparency on this definition, and increase data collection on the level and frequency of force used in police interactions with the public. The committee also agrees that any country's failure to publish a complete annual count of persons killed by police undermines the ROL.

LEVELS OF ANALYSIS AND CAUSES OF EXCESSIVE FORCE

Social science scholars have long debated whether a range of social and political phenomena result from structures, institutions, rules, and processes that determine and constrain individuals' choices, or from individual agency. Although the "structure vs. agency" debate may seem like a mere academic matter, it is particularly important when considering the drivers of police use of force. This distinction is relevant to assess the many interventions that are aimed at minimizing police use of force. Do officers resort to the use of force because of individual decisions related to individual characteristics, knowledge, and experiences? Or do officers' use of force depend on institutional structures such as formal legal rules, administrative procedures, and organizational norms?

The answers to these questions are of fundamental importance for designing use-of-force policies and training programs. Accordingly, when assessing research about police use of force, one must be attentive to the level of analysis.

Individual studies often focus on one level. For instance, Ba and colleagues (2021) examine individual characteristics, like race and gender, as determinants of officer decisions to use force. Owens and colleagues (2018), on the other hand, highlight the importance of organizational practices—a modified supervisory strategy to model procedural justice and encourage "slowing down" officers' thought processes—to minimize police use of force. Meanwhile, Magaloni and Rodriguez (2020) signal the significance of macro-level policies as drivers of police use of force; both in terms of increased use, resulting from militarized security operations in Mexico, and reduced use, after restricting the practice of confessions as evidence in criminal trials.

As these studies suggest, police use of force is a multi-faceted issue. In assessing evidence regarding approaches to minimize use of force, it is important to consider the factors across multiple levels (from national laws to individuals' characteristics) that may cause use of force to vary, and to determine whether the appropriate interventions to address it ought to target individual officers, the organization, or macro-level policy change, as well as the interaction among all three.

SOCIETAL ATTITUDES TOWARD POLICE VIOLENCE

The police are a key entity of the state authorized to use force for legitimate purposes in regard to promoting the ROL, responding to crime, and protecting the population (Bayley, 1985). As such, the use of force is a central factor in shaping citizen support and trust of police, and the state more broadly. Scholars have found public support for unconstrained use of force by police in some countries in response to high crime rates, including in South Africa (Smith, 2019), Brazil (Ahnen, 2007), and the Philippines (Tusalem, 2019). Public popularity has in turn been an effective electoral strategy, with politicians promising aggressive approaches to addressing crime often finding electoral success (Holland, 2013).

But recent scholarly research has also shown that routine police abuse of its authority to use force comes at a cost and may well undermine public support and legitimacy. In the Central American context, Cruz (2015) finds that police misconduct, including physical abuse, erodes public support for police and government overall. Looking at Costa Rica, Gingerich and Oliveros (2018) find that observing police violence makes citizens less willing to report crime to the police. Scholars have similarly examined the relationship between police violence and willingness to cooperate with the police in the United States. A study by Desmond and colleagues (2016) found that a high-profile case of police misconduct in Milwaukee led to fewer 911 calls, particularly among Black residents. Although this study's analysis has been called into question (Zoorob, 2020), a recent working paper by Ang and colleagues (2021) draws on a comparison between ShotSpotter data and 911 calls in eight U.S. cities which found a drop in 911 calls following the high-profile killing of George Floyd by Minneapolis police. Scholars have also shown that public perceptions of police can change in response to police violence. González (2020) showed that the proportion of citizens in São Paulo, Brazil, that considered the state's police to be "too violent" rose from 44 to 73 percent immediately following widely broadcasted footage of police use of excessive force. Notably, scholars have also shown that changes in public attitudes do not occur uniformly across the population. In the context of Uganda, Curtice (2021) draws on evidence from a natural experiment to demonstrate that public perceptions of police became more negative following police repression, with the greatest effect among regime opponents. In the United States, Jefferson and colleagues (2021) similarly find differences in perceptions of officer-involved shootings by race.

Taken together, these studies suggest that, while public support for police taking a more aggressive stance to curb crime and violence may pose an obstacle to efforts to minimize police use of force, excessive and unlawful use of force by police not only undermines the ROL, it may also reduce public support and cooperation.

ORGANIZATION OF THE REPORT

Following this introduction, Chapter 2 reviews common approaches aimed at minimizing police use of force. It captures background information on laws and standards for police use of force, external oversight bodies, training, internal accountability, technologies, and administrative incentives. This chapter in large part summarizes the findings and examples presented to the committee in the commissioned papers. Chapter 3 offers the committee's shared understanding of the state of knowledge regarding police policies and practices for the use of force. It also provides recommendations for international donors and reasonable steps forward to minimize the level of force used by police, identifies data needs, and focuses on use of force policies, training, and accountability mechanisms. The Appendix provides biographical sketches of committee members and study staff.

2

Practices Designed to Regulate and Control Use of Force

In its first report, this committee laid out a framework for evidence-based policing—the review, assessment, translation, and application of scientifically derived knowledge as well as processes to strengthen police departments' decision-making, actions, and overall agency functioning. An evidence-based approach to policing requires: (1) a reliable body of knowledge about policing practices; (2) the ongoing practice of evidence-based and systematic targeting, testing, and tracking in policing; and (3) the institutionalization and implementation of knowledge in police practice (NASEM, 2021, p. 2). Concerning police use of force, it is envisioned that evidence-based policing practices and reforms will complement efforts through international law and human rights bodies to reduce the use of force and violence by the police as well as improving policing generally.

To aid in accumulating a reliable body of knowledge, the committee considers different efforts and research findings from studies of policies and practices aimed at minimizing use of excessive force by police. The different strategies described in the commissioned papers and workshop can be divided into six categories: laws and standards, external oversight bodies, police training, internal accountability and control mechanisms, technologies, and administrative incentives (outlined in Cano, 2021).

While insightful, many of the existing studies have methodological and contextual limitations that could affect their applicability to policing contexts in other countries. However, this should primarily be interpreted as an absence of rigorous evidence or lack of external validity, rather than evidence for a particular strategy's inadequacy. Several policies and practices are promising in that they have strong theoretical groundings (and at times—strong internal validity) and have shown some limited success in practice or through rigorous evaluation.

The committee emphasizes that these promising approaches require further testing and evaluation, as required by an evidence-based approach to policing. Promising approaches, when implemented, must be evaluated with attention to systematically measuring outcomes, as well as unintended consequences, across time (short-, medium-, and long-term). They need to be continuously assessed, and implementing agencies and funders need to be ready to adapt and change course based on those assessments if warranted. See further discussion on an evidence-based approach and evaluation of promising approaches to police training in the committee's first two reports (NASEM, 2021; 2022). This chapter provides background on common approaches to minimizing police use of force, drawing heavily on studies and insights presented in the commissioned papers (Alpert et al., 2021; Cano, 2021) and the workshop discussion, and sets the stage for the committee's conclusions and recommendations in Chapter 3.

LAWS AND STANDARDS

A basic way to control police use of force is through the law, specifically the application of the law by the courts against police officers who exceed reasonable standards of using force or who use force illegally. There are also international guidelines for policing that regulate police use of force and codes of conduct, and these have served as a framework for national and local standards and policies and for assessments of human rights violations. While the existence of laws that place boundaries on acceptable uses of force may or may not affect those uses in practice, creating a transparent definition of when and how force should, and should not, be used is a necessary first step. Such a definition is needed to distinguish between force that is excessive, such as firing into a crowd of peaceful protestors, from force that is both justified and promotes the rule of law (ROL), such as incapacitating an active shooter.

International Standards and Guidelines

Several declarations and principles support international human rights standards that can also be used by states to develop use-of-force policies. For example, the Universal Declaration of Human Rights, the International Covenant on Civil and Political Rights, and the Convention against Torture all provide guidance and benchmarks for how police and other law enforcement authorities should treat citizens. While the United Nations (UN) Basic Principles on the Use of Force and Firearms (hereafter, UN Basic Principles) acknowledge that in certain limited circumstances law enforcement officials may need to use force, the principles also detail how in such instances force must be carried out in compliance with international human rights law (Biernert et al., 2015). Relatedly, the UN International Human Rights Standards for Law Enforcement on the use of force include the following:

- Everyone has the right to life, security of the person, and freedom from torture, cruel, inhuman, or degrading treatment and punishment;
- Non-violent means are to be attempted first;
- Force is to be used only when strictly necessary;
- Force is to be used only for lawful law enforcement purposes;
- No exceptions or excuses shall be allowed for unlawful use of force;
- Use of force is to be always proportional to lawful objectives;
- Restraint is to be exercised in the use of force;
- Damage and injury are to be minimized;
- A range of means for differentiated use of force is to be made available;
- All officers are to be trained in the use of the various means for differentiated use of force; and
- All officers are to be trained in use of non-violent means.
(United Nations High Commissioner for Human Rights, 1997, p. 7)

The UN Code of Conduct for Law Enforcement Officials, adopted in 1979, says officers can only use force as a last resort, and that force should be proportional to the legitimate goal of the officer (United Nations, 1979). The Code of Conduct also emphasizes that police officers should uphold the human rights of all citizens and seek medical attention for all persons as necessary. Similarly, the European Convention on Human Rights permits force only when "absolutely necessary" and ensures that citizens have the right to peaceful assembly without restrictions (European Court of Human Rights, 2021). The UN Basic Principles specify that law enforcement officials shall not use firearms against persons except in self-defense or the defense of others against the imminent threat of death or serious injury. These principles are also outlined in the UN Guidance on Less-Lethal Weapons in Law Enforcement.[1] In a workshop presentation to the committee, Flores (2021) summed up these international standards by cataloging them under four overarching principles: legality, necessity, proportionality, and accountability (see Box 2-1).

UN human rights treaty monitoring bodies can provide guidance and recommendations to member states for relatively technical modifications to regulations. These modifications can, in theory, provide a legal basis for

---

[1] Available: https://www.ohchr.org/sites/default/files/Documents/HRBodies/CCPR/LLW_Guidance.pdf.

> **BOX 2-1**
> **Four Key International Human Rights Law Principles on Use of Deadly Force**
> **(Workshop Presentation)**
>
> **Legality**
> Concerning any lethal force policy:
> - It must be based on a law enacted by a legislature at the national or subnational level;
> - It must comply with international human rights standards; and
> - While it authorizes police use of deadly force, it must also clearly limit it.
>
> **Necessity**
> Lethal use of force must be necessary, meaning it must be responsive to an immediate, particularized threat and only be used as a last resort.
>
> **Proportionality**
> - The use of force must always be proportionate to the threat the officer confronts and weighed against the fundamental human rights of the individual.
> - Lethal force must only be used in response to an equal threat of death or serious bodily injury to the officer or other people.
>
> **Accountability**
> - Law enforcement must issue a full report to an independent, external oversight body for each instance of the use of lethal force, regardless of the outcome.
> - Police departments must be transparent about use of force policies and practices.
>
> SOURCE: Flores, 2021.

pushing practice in a direction to align policing with human rights principles. The UN Human Rights Council also conducts a Universal Periodic Review, which includes a review of human rights records for all member states (United Nations Human Rights Council, 2020). This review is a universal mechanism that can serve as an accountability mechanism for countries with human rights violations within police forces.[2] Similarly, the

---

[2]For example, the Committee Against Torture (CAT) at the UN High Commission on Human Rights, in relation to ongoing investigations of police torture of more than 100 African American men in Chicago during the 1970s and 1980s, instructed that the United States "should promptly, thoroughly and impartially investigate all allegations of acts of torture by law enforcement personnel and bring perpetrators to justice" (UN Committee Against Torture, 2006).

Inter-American Commission on Human Rights monitors human rights violations by the police on a more case by case basis (see Box 2-2).

These international structures serve to call attention to pervasive issues that may go unaddressed at individual jurisdiction or precinct levels. Here we highlight three examples of issues regarding policing impact on minority communities, lack of swift investigation, and shortcomings in sufficient and independent investigations of police-involved killings.

In 2021, the UN Human Rights Council (2021) released a report calling for policing reforms to address systemic racism affecting people of African descent worldwide.[3] This report highlighted that racism was not simply an individual officer problem but could be found within policing systems. Thus, systemic racism within policing cannot be remedied by training or correcting individual officers but only by reforming those systems in policing that can create disparate or discriminatory outcomes.

In 2009, the European Court of Human Rights ruled in the case of *Iribarren Pinillos v. Spain* that Spain had violated the prohibition of inhuman or degrading treatment and the right to a fair trial within a reasonable time. The Court considered that the use of a smoke bomb thrown by national police created risk to physical injury and death to those present and that a determination on whether the use was necessary and proportionate in the circumstances was never established. The Court found that failure of the Spanish judicial system to conduct an effective and timely investigation into the incident violated both the European Convention on Human Rights Article 3, prohibition of torture, and Article 6, right to a fair trial within a reasonable time, given that the proceedings had lasted almost 12 years.

In 2017, the Inter-American Court of Human Rights ruled on Brazil for the case of Nova Brasilia, police operations in a neighborhood in Rio de Janeiro in 1994 and 1995 that resulted in a number of citizen deaths. The court found that early investigations did not guarantee independence and impartiality. In its judgment, the Court determined that: (1) Brazil had to conduct effective investigations into these events and publish annual reports on deaths in police operations with information on the resulting investigations; and (2) the State of Rio de Janeiro had to introduce policies and goals to reduce deaths in police encounters (Inter-American Court of Human Rights, 2017). In June 2021, the same court determined that the State of Venezuela must also publish similar annual reports, as part of its sentencing in the case of *Guerrero, Molina and others v. Venezuela* (Inter-American Court of Human Rights, 2021). While these actions suggest that there may be scope for international norms to regulate police use of force, the impact of UN evaluations or these court orders on police use of force has not been empirically evaluated.

---

[3] See https://www.ohchr.org/en/NewsEvents/Pages/DisplayNews.aspx?NewsID=27296&LangID=E.

> **BOX 2-2**
> **The Inter-American Commission on Human Rights**
>
> The Inter-American Commission on Human Rights is an autonomous body of the Organization of American States, whose mission is to promote and protect human rights in the western hemisphere. To fulfill this mandate, the commission offers three main mechanisms that may be taken advantage of in pursuit of justice.
>
> It may consider petitions from individuals who claim their rights have been violated by the state and that they have been unable to find justice in their own country. The commission brings together the petitioner and the state to "explore a friendly settlement." If such an outcome is not possible, the commission may recommend specific measures, or may report the case to the Inter-American Court of Human Rights.
>
> In addition, persons who believe they are at particular risk of having their rights infringed may make an urgent appeal to the commission, which can call on a state to take "precautionary measures" to prevent irreparable harm.
>
> Additionally, the commission conducts on-site visits to assess and report on the human rights situation of a country, then issue recommendations for action. In recent years (2020, 2021) the visits have included analysis of the repression of social protests in Latin America during the pandemic with instances of disproportionate use of force by the police. The commission also noted in some instances considerable differences between official statistics of persons injured and Non-governmental Organizations (NGOs') counts. The recommendations included the establishment of consistent, updated, transparent, and public registries of information about human rights violations with the participation of the civil society to avoid disparities between official statistics and NGOs' counts of injured persons that undermine the public confidence in the police, the criminal justice system, and in general the government and democracy itself.

National Laws Related to Use of Force

Several countries have introduced new laws or guidelines that define acceptable uses of force by police. Peru, for instance, issued a legislative decree in 2015 to regulate the use of force by the National Police, which contains and develops relevant international principles. Likewise, the Brazilian government published inter-ministerial guidelines in 2019 to the same effect, though only binding for federal police forces. In South Africa, the *Marikana Panel Report*, produced by an official commission after review of deaths in a police encounter in Marikana in 2012, recommended that the state consider the Model Bill for Use of Force by Police and other law enforcement agencies in South Africa, which had been proposed by civil society organizations, as a suitable starting point for new legislation (Panel of Experts on Policing and Crowd Management, 2018, p. 132). In the United States, the 1985 Supreme Court case *Tennesee v. Garner* held that laws authorizing police use of deadly force to apprehend fleeing, unarmed, and nondangerous suspects were unconstitutional.

The U.S. ruling is notable because, following this decision, homicides committed by police officers nationwide fell by approximately 16 percent, with evidence suggesting that the reduction is due not only to a reduction in fleeing felons but also to a general reduction in police shootings (Tennenbaum, 1994). This case illustrates the effect that national policy decisions can have on police behavior.

Many countries have adopted laws that reflect the UN General Assembly principle of Necessity, summarized in Box 2-1. The following examples illustrate this concept according to various police codes:

- *Cyprus*: Police Code of Ethics, 2003 Art. 32: "The Police use force only when strictly necessary and only to the extent required to obtain a legitimate objective";
- *Kenya*: National Police Service Act No. 11A, 2011 Sixth Schedule, A(1), p. 62: "A police officer shall always attempt to use non-violent means first and force may only be employed when non-violent means are ineffective or without any promise of achieving the intended result"; and
- *Greece*: Code of Police Ethics, 2004 Art. 2(e): "The Police personnel ... shall use non-violent means while maintaining and enforcing law. The use of force is, in theory, permitted only when absolutely necessary and to the extent envisaged and required for law enforcement. The use of force shall always respect the principles of necessity, adequacy and proportionality" (Biernert et al., 2015).

However, the committee notes that simply adopting UN guidelines as local or national laws is not always feasible or desirable. This is particularly true when strong norms or practical on-the-ground realities conflict with the UN standards as written. As a result, guidelines may need to be adjusted to fit the needs of the community at hand. Box 2-3 provides an example of how international standards can be translated to local context with some success.

Moving beyond a focus on necessity, some countries and municipalities around the world offer specific guidance on when the use of force can be justified by on-duty officers, including situations where the deployment of weapons, notably firearms, could be limited, such as in the following examples:

- *Mexico*: Law on the use of force by law enforcement in the Federal District, 2008 Art. 9, lists the following situations in which force may be used: "in the submission of a person resisting arrest following the order of a competent authority or after having committed a breach of a law or regulation, in fulfilling a duty or lawful order

> **BOX 2-3**
> **Translating Standards to Regional and National Levels**
> **(Workshop Presentation)**
>
> While the available international standards and mechanisms are not always easily transferred to state or regional contexts, there are ongoing efforts to achieve this translation. For example, the African Policing Civilian Oversight Forum (APCOF) has used international standards to develop regional standard operating procedures and guidelines on police use of force for the East African Police Commissioners Co Operation Organization (EAPCCO). This interpretation of global standards to a local level is important, as it builds ownership and enables the standards and guidelines to be implemented in ways that are more likely to resonate with local context and practical needs and challenges. These procedures and guidelines developed for EAPCCO focus on five areas of operating procedures that interface with use of force: stop-and-search, arrest and detention, use of force generally, assemblies, and conducting interviews.
>
> APCOF also builds dissemination into their process to ensure consistency and coherence among standards from an international level down through to a regional, country, or local level. Probert (2018) examined the utility of this approach of local country translation of a continental standard (The African Commissions Guidelines on the Policing of Assemblies by Law Enforcement officials in Africa) into training in Malawi. Albeit modest, the outcomes of this study indicated a slight increase in acceptance among police officers of the public's right of assembly, a core idea within the guidelines. Probert (2018) also found that the extent to which officers believed procedural irregularities were sufficient to disrupt an assembly was diminished after the training.
>
> SOURCE: Tait, 2021.

given by a competent authority, in the prevention of unlawful acts in the protection or defense of legally protected interests, or as legitimate self-defense" (Amnesty International, 2015, p. 23).

- *Indonesia*: INP Regulation No. 8/2009 Art. 47 provides that "[t]he use of firearms shall be allowed only if strictly necessary to preserve human life" (Biernert et al., 2015).

International standards and guidelines attempt to put boundaries on police use of force and define when that force may be considered excessive, while national laws codifying a reasonable amount of force and when it can be used vary by country. How standards and guidelines are translated into regional or local laws and directives, and how these translations are in turn effective in controlling police use of force, both could benefit from further examination. The effectiveness of laws and standards ties directly to the extent to which they are enforced. Obstacles to enforcement—whether they be lack of resources to implement legal requirements, lack of training on the standards and laws, or purposeful neglect—can be investigated and addressed by the oversight and accountability strategies discussed below.

EXTERNAL OVERSIGHT BODIES

The committee was also presented with information on different structures for external oversight. Informative examples include: the Independent Commission of Investigations (INDECOM) in Jamaica, Police Complaints Authorities (PCAs) in India, Police Ombudsman Office (Ouvidoria da Polícia) in Brazil, the Independent Police Investigative Directory (IPID) in South Africa, the Independent Policing Oversight Authority (IPOA) in Kenya, and consent decrees and civilian review boards in the United States.

The INDECOM is a good example of an external oversight body. Jamaica instituted it in 2010 in response to an infamous case of multiple killings by police and the army in the Tivoli Gardens neighborhood in Kingston (INDECOM, 2020). INDECOM was tasked to independently investigate serious allegations against police. In principle, INDECOM had full control over investigations of police shootings and deaths in custody. INDECOM claims that, as a result of its work, deaths in police shootings diminished slightly at first, from 733 in the three-year period before its creation to 687 in the first three years of its existence, and then declined sharply to 327 in the following three years, after it established working protocols and awareness sessions. Even though a causal relationship between the establishment of INDECOM and reductions in police shootings cannot be drawn from existing evaluations, and other factors, such as a reversion to previous practices after an abnormally violent few years, may play a role, the declining trends in shootings warrants further study.

Hu and Conrad (2020) found that court-ordered accountability institutions can decrease unremanded deaths in police custody.[4] A 2006 judgment by the Supreme Court of India required states and districts to establish

---

[4]The Hu and Conrad study referenced two types of police custodial deaths: (1) deaths remanded to police custody, and (2) deaths not remanded to police custody. The former refers to the death of individuals sent back to police custody by an Indian court for the purpose of furthering an investigation; the latter refers to the death of individuals taken into custody by police officers prior to a court appearance. When an individual is remanded to police custody by an Indian court, one can expect the court to pay heightened attention to the physical security of that individual. As such, the police are likely to be more constrained in their use of violence against these individuals. As expected, the count of custodial deaths not remanded to police by the court is larger than the count of custodial deaths remanded to police custody following legal action. Because police violence is more prevalent in cases where individuals are taken into initial police custody than when they are remanded to police by an Indian court, this study uses a count of unremanded police custodial deaths as the main measure of police violence (Hu and Conrad, 2020).

local PCAs. These court-ordered, regional bodies were created to allow citizens to report allegations of police abuse, by which police officers can be monitored—and potentially held accountable—for abuses of power. Using a difference-in-difference research design that uses state-level variations when PCAs were adopted, Hu and Conrad (2020) found that from 2001 to 2015, Indian police officers were less likely to engage in behaviors that violated human rights when these oversight bodies were created. These findings align with general human rights literature on what works for national human rights institutions: formal institutional safeguards can be effective even in authoritarian and transition regimes, and complaint-handling mandates help institutions build broad bases of support (Linos and Pegram, 2017).

Conversely, however, the creation of external monitoring bodies in Brazil, South Africa, and Kenya appears to have had little effect on the use of force by officers. In 1995, the state of São Paulo, Brazil, created a Police Ombudsman Office (*Ouvidoria da Polícia*), which received confidential complaints against the police from the general public and addressed them to the relevant bodies: the Internal Affairs Unit (*Corregedoria*) or the Prosecutor's Office. The ombudsman had no investigative powers. Many other Brazilian states followed suit during the late 1990s and early 2000s (Lemgruber, 2002). Though there are no robust impact evaluations of these oversight bodies, in Brazil the creation of *Ouvidorias* did not appear to coincide with a reduction in police abuses, which Lemgruber and colleagues (2003) hypothesize is due to the *Ouvidorias'* lack of investigative capacity and reliance on previously existing internal controls.

In South Africa, the IPID came into operation on April 1, 2012, and was mandated to investigate serious cases of police misconduct and all civilian deaths in which officers were involved. If allegations were substantiated, the case either transferred to the National Prosecuting Authority, if criminal in nature, or to the police with disciplinary recommendations (APCOF, 2017). The IPID's predecessor, the Independent Complaints Directorate (ICD), came into operation in 1997. The ICD was only required to investigate deaths in police custody and deaths as a result of police action, so the IPID was designed as a replacement (Bruce, 2020). While the IDC also had a general responsibility to receive complaints against the police, it could refer these to the police to allow for internal investigation by the police. Muntingh and Dereymaeker (2013) and Bruce (2020) argue that the creation of the IPID, while more powerful than its predecessor and with obligations to investigate serious allegations of criminal offenses, provided the South African Police Service with an apparent justification for not being internally accountable for its use of force (i.e., for relaxing its own internal controls, given that there would be an external body charged with oversight).

In Kenya, IPOA is charged with investigating deaths and serious injuries caused by police actions (Gandhi et al., 2021). It can refer criminal cases, its main focus, to the Office of the Director of Public Prosecutions. IPOA is also mandated with monitoring the Internal Affairs Unit investigations and can take them over if it believes the IAU is being delayed or unreasonable. In other words, it has the additional mandate of overseeing internal controls. However, this depends on the cooperation from the police, and although the police are legally bound to inform IPOA about deaths in police actions, in practice many cases are not reported, which seriously compromises its oversight capability (Gandhi et al., 2021).

Recent research has pointed to the influence the judicial system has on policing practices. Magaloni and Rodriguez (2020) show empirically through statistical analysis of data from the National Survey of the Population Deprived of Liberty, collected by the Mexican National Statistics Agency, how greater judicial oversight of police and prosecutors introduced through the abandonment of the inquisitorial system in Mexico led to a reduction in torture of suspects by police. This paper supports the notion that norms and incentives within the criminal justice system can affect police use of force and that adjustment to policing behavior requires institutional design or reform. While more research is needed to trace the progression of jurisprudence and the behavior of courts on procedural rights in criminal trials, the research by Magaloni and Rodriguez (2020) advocates that the introduction of stronger judicial checks on prosecutors and police is essential to restrain abuse. In another example, a study examined a supreme court order to halt police operations in the favelas in Rio de Janeiro and found a 66 percent decrease in persons killed by police, accompanied by decreases in police shootings and injuries resulting from shootings; a secondary effect of the order on police operations was a sharp decrease in homicides and shootings between citizens (Bullock, 2021).

In the United States, a consent decree is a form of federal oversight of local police—a court-ordered agreement between law enforcement agencies and government to address a problem. There is some correlational evidence that consent decrees and other forms of structural reform litigation may have been effective in reducing misconduct (see e.g., Chanin 2015, 2017; Goh, 2020; Harmon, 2009; Rushin, 2014, 2015). After reviewing the evaluation research conducted on consent decrees, Chillar (2021, p. 7) concludes that the timing of many studies (e.g., while an agency is still under the decree or recently released from it) does not allow for understanding the long-term impacts of consent decrees. Almost all of the cited studies note that, in the absence of continuing oversight, the organizational changes that occurred during consent decrees were at high risk of reverting back to previous practices.

Civilian review boards have also gained popularity in the United States as another type of external monitoring body. The Council on Criminal

Justice's Task Force on Policing (2021) reviewed a variety of models of civilian oversight and concluded that rigorous empirical research and relative merits of oversight models do not exist. Specifically, their report reviews the most influential studies and notes many methodological problems, including the lack of accounting for other policy changes during the research periods. Thus, while there are good theoretical reasons to assume that civilian oversight may offer promising aspects such as improving public relations and transparency, the committee is unaware of any robust empirical evidence evaluating the effectiveness of these oversight bodies on police use of force.

There is some evidence from different countries to suggest that when external monitoring bodies are given investigatory and disciplinary powers and strong internal monitoring mechanisms, they may be more effective in reducing the use of force than bodies that lack these characteristics. As with other approaches to reducing the use of force, there is not yet a body of empirical evidence to support the effectiveness of external monitoring bodies. Future research could be beneficial for developing a better understanding of the role of external oversight bodies and whether they can support internal efforts to train police officers and provide reliable accountability mechanisms.

POLICE TRAINING AND EVALUATIONS

In the second report (NASEM, 2022), the committee reached a consensus on five connected principles of police training that are grounded in an evidence-based approach and that can support the ROL and the protection of the public. Training that prepares officers to reasonably use force when necessary must dissuade officers from resorting to excessive force. The five principles, which are interconnected, are as follows:

1. *Training must do no harm.* This first principle is fundamental to developing training that controls police use of force. Training must not only focus on the evidence about what is effective in protecting the public and promoting the ROL, it must also not contribute to greater abuses, harm, or other negative consequences at a population level. The committee understands that legitimate use of force by police can injure or kill individuals posing threats but underscores that training that leads to excessive use of force can damage whole communities without crime-reducing or public order benefits. The uses of training must be monitored for positive outcomes, negative consequences, and misuses. The remaining principles operationalize this goal.
2. *The content of training should be based on the best available evidence.* The policing strategies, tactics, knowledge, and skills that

officers are trained in should be supported by evidence showing that they are effectively linked to *both* supporting the ROL *and* protecting the public. Existing scientific knowledge and scientific approaches can help identify effective policing strategies and activities in which officers should be trained.
3. *Training must also use evidence-based methods.* The educational methods and styles of teaching used to deliver training should also be selected based on evidence of impact. Finding effective ways for officers to learn, apply knowledge, and update that knowledge is essential in linking training to everyday practices, behaviors, and outcomes.
4. *Police agencies must continuously gather new evidence about the impact of training content and methods* by tracking, testing, and evaluating ongoing training efforts for implementation and outcomes.
5. *The delivery of training needs to be flexible and contextualized* given the resources, cultures, and capacities of different police agencies that INL supports.

There is some evidence from the United States that police training may reduce the rate at which police use force in the field. Some of this evidence is based on the procedural justice model of policing, which emphasizes transparency, responding to community concerns, and explaining police actions (Wood et al., 2020). Procedural justice training teaches officers to give community members an opportunity to explain their actions and to describe the legal bases for officers' responses to those actions (Council on Criminal Justice, 2021). Procedural justice training promotes respectful encounters between community members and police officers with the goals of enhancing police legitimacy and perceptions of fairness, and building community trust in the police. Continual training programs focused on procedural justice have been evaluated in Seattle (Owens et al., 2018) using a randomized controlled trial (RCT), as well as in Chicago (Papachristos, 2015) and Camden (Goh, 2021) using credible quasi-experimental variation in the roll-out of training programs. In all these evaluations, the programs appear to have reduced the rate at which officers used force. A recent RCT conducted in 120 crime hot spots within three U.S. cities examined the effect of procedural justice training on police behavior (Weisburd et al., 2022). The study found a reduction in arrests for officers who received the training compared to those that did not. Further, through pre- and post-training surveys to households, it found that citizens in areas patrolled by officers who received the training were less likely to perceive officers as using unnecessary force.

There is also some evidence that de-escalation training[5] may reduce use of force incidents. Most de-escalation training emphasizes strategies for the prevention and management of aggression, including training in early intervention, verbal and non-verbal interaction or communication styles, the selection of appropriate responses in potentially violent encounters, and the use of physical intervention techniques, all designed to reduce conflict, aggression, injuries, and violence during police encounters (Engel et al., 2017). Engel and colleagues' evaluation of the Police Executive Research Forum's Integrating Communications, Assessment, and Tactics (ICAT) de-escalation training program used a stepped-wedge design to limit contamination issues and found the results demonstrated statistically significant reductions in use of force incidents, citizen injuries, and officer injuries in the post-training period (Engel et al., 2022).

An RCT studying a customized de-escalation program in Tempe, Arizona, found that according to officer surveys, post training, officers placed greater emphasis on compromise and self-reported greater use of compromise, knowing when to walk away, and maintaining officer safety (White and Orosco, 2021). Results from phone surveys of hundreds of citizens with recent encounters with Tempe officers reflected statistically significant differences between officers exposed to the training and officers in the control group, all favoring a positive training impact (White and Orosco, 2021). Findings regarding use of force were inconclusive given confounding issues of the pandemic and protests during the study; though the researchers did observe, through analysis of body-worn-camera footage, a significant reduction in citizens injured in use of force incidents for officers who received the training. Of note, the results of this RCT are based on surveys (captured attitudes) and not subsequent behaviors on the job.

An ethnographic case study of de-escalation training, presented at the workshop, suggested that training officers on threat assessment and slower thought processes in high-stress situations may reduce the rate at which they use indiscriminate force (Espinoza, 2021). Officers who do not know how they are expected to respond to perceived threats cannot be expected to use force in a way that is consistent with the ROL. Training which thoroughly explains to officers the boundaries of their agency's use of force policy, and how far the organization can legally go to defend them, can

---

[5]Forms of de-escalation training have varied across agencies and jurisdictions. One specific definition of police de-escalation exists within the 2017 National Consensus Policy and Discussion Paper on Use of Force (a collaborative effort among 11 law enforcement leadership and labor organizations in the United States). This definition states that police de-escalation is "taking action or communicating verbally or non-verbally during a potential force encounter in an attempt to stabilize the situation and reduce the immediacy of the threat so that more time, options, and resources can be called upon to resolve the situation without the use of force or with a reduction in the force necessary" (National Consensus Policy, 2020, p. 2).

provide critical context regarding the extent to which they may use force on the job. Espinoza (2021) observed that officers who know and take ownership of use-of-force regulations are more likely to make choices consistent with the ROL (Espinoza, 2021).

While promising, these studies have been limited to a few contexts, notably cities in the United States. It is therefore unclear whether similar effects would be observed when conducting such de-escalation trainings in different contexts.

The evidence base for effective police training to minimize use of force is therefore still quite limited. Most police training programs are not evaluated in ways that allow for rigorous assessment of the effectiveness of the training in controlling police use of force. This is frequently because of institutional restrictions within the police department that prevent researchers from linking police training to recorded police actions in the community. Instead, training is most commonly evaluated based on officer performance in simulation studies, or self-reported attitudes, which are subjected to various biases (e.g., social desirability bias and experimenter demand effects). In order to create an evidence base on effective training regarding police use of force, data on how much force police actually use must be collected in a way that can be linked with the training (or other such policy interventions). This includes implementing training programs in a way that allows for empirical data collection and evaluation. See Box 2-4 for a description of data linkages and levels of aggregation for evaluating training.

RCTs are generally considered to be the "gold standard" for producing causal evidence on the impact of a training, policy, or strategy. In a successful RCT, the researcher exposes people, or groups of people, to a treatment, randomly (e.g., via coin flip). When a random assignment process is the only thing that determines who is treated, any difference in average outcomes across control and treatment group can be causally attributed to the treatment.

RCTs are not always feasible or ethical. Sometimes, however, the implementation of a policy can create situations where treatment is arbitrary or "as good as random" and allow for natural experiments to be conducted in real time or after an implementation event. The most important characteristic of these natural experiments is that the treatment assignment rule is known to the researcher, and specifically known to be unrelated to the factors that can affect the outcomes of interest. Good examples of this include the adoption of a militarized policing after a close electoral win (used to study the impact of police militarization in Mexico (Dell, 2015) and the distribution of federal grants for hiring (used to study the impact of police manpower) (Evans and Owens, 2007). A bad example of this would be examining the effectiveness of a new code enforcement policy by comparing tax compliance across jurisdictions—some with codes in

BOX 2-4
Linking Training to Police Actions

Assessments of the impact of a training program or policy can be direct and individualized or measured at higher levels of aggregation. Both approaches can provide useful information about what works in promoting the ROL, but having data available at the individual trainee level allows for more flexibility in what can be analyzed.

There are two types of data linkages, which can be thought of as cross-sectional and temporal. The most aggregated cross-sectional link is national—showing, for example, that country A has adopted a particular training program and country B has not. Differentiating between states or jurisdictions within country A and country B that have or have not adopted a training program allows researchers to link the training program data with state- or jurisdiction-level information on crime, use of police force, or economic participation. Individual level data on actions or characteristics on officers are the most disaggregated.

Cross-sectional data links can sometimes occur both within and across aggregation levels. For example, if training information is identified at the officer level, that training information could be linked to other individual records on use of force. If an individual record also contains a more aggregated cross-sectional link, for example the jurisdiction employing the officer, that individual data can be linked to jurisdiction level policies. Since the state or country in which a particular district is located is generally public information, aggregating district links to the state or country level is a trivial task.

Temporal data links refer to the time-frame when an event occurred or policy was implemented. They can be annual, monthly, or even as disaggregated as the minute (such as the moment that a call for service was received by a dispatcher). When temporal links are more aggregated (e.g., annual or monthly data), it can be more difficult to determine if an event followed or preceded a training program or intervention.

Disaggregated links can allow for more precise estimates of causal effects. However, from a policy analysis perspective, it is most important to be able to accurately link a program or practice to outcomes at a level that is conceptually meaningful. On one hand, a policy that provides an officer with less than lethal weaponry might be expected to affect the amount of deadly forced used by that officer—in such a case, an individualized cross-sectional link would be the most informative level of linking.

On the other hand, a training program intended to encourage officers to intervene when they observe out-of-policy behavior by their colleagues might be expected to affect use of force at a higher level of cross-sectional aggregation—uses of force by individual officers that cannot be linked to an officer's peer group (e.g., the beat assignment) might actually be less informative than use of force data where the cross-sectional link is aggregated to the district level.

Causal estimates can frequently be made with fewer assumptions when data are linked at a more disaggregate level. There are, of course, costs associated with collecting linked data; these include financial, political, and privacy constraints, particularly when the recorded data are potentially sensitive (e.g., individualized cross-sectional links for officers involved in fatal encounters). Organizations will have to weigh these costs against the value of collecting as much information as possible for reliable analysis of training, policy, or strategy impacts.

place charging policing units with addressing revenue shortfalls caused by tax evasion and some that decided this wasn't an issue. In this case, treatment assignment is determined by how much of a problem the outcome of interest was believed to be; places with varying levels of concern about tax evasion will generally have different rates of tax evasion, with or without a responsive policy. This is frequently referred to as "confounding" of treatment effects. Unfortunately, when confounding is present, the results of a study can be larger than or even the wrong direction of the true treatment effect, and there are limited diagnostic tools for figuring out how large a problem confounding is, when present (LaLonde, 1986).

At the same time, just because random assignment occurred does not necessarily mean that observed difference in outcomes between treated and control groups is the effect of the policy; it is possible that two groups of people will have different outcomes due to chance (which can be thought of as "random" confounding). This is particularly a concern when the number of units in each group is small. In addition, the context in which an RCT is implemented could influence measured effects. For example, in some police departments beat officers may have better lines of communication with their supervisors, which can affect how a community policing policy is implemented in practice. This would mean that a perfectly implemented RCT of community policing across divisions of one well-integrated department would have a different effect than the same policy studied in a department with less communication (Blair et al., 2021). Attempting to replicate RCTs in different contexts can address both issues of "random" confounding and context-specific effects. It is important to note that replicating confounded non-experimental studies is not guaranteed to produce unbiased causal effects, unless there is good reason to believe that the confounding issue is, itself, randomly distributed across studies—and this is rarely the case.

BARRIERS TO INTERNAL CONTROL MECHANISMS

Many police agencies have internal affairs units or other internal control mechanisms that monitor officer behavior and formally handle accusations that arise against officer use of force. The effectiveness of these internal control and accountability mechanisms is far from guaranteed. For example, effectiveness can be limited by cultural norms within the organization, by a weak system of complaints processing and tracking, or by a lack of the supervision necessary to activate such controls when a violation has occurred.

A significant hindrance to promoting ethical and accountable policing is the existence of a "code of silence" within police organizations, which prevents officers from reporting the problematic behavior of other officers to internal control mechanisms or their supervisors. The phrase "code of silence" refers to both the reluctance of police officers to report corrupt activities carried out by their fellow officers and the reluctance of police administrators to acknowledge the existence of corruption within their agencies. In its investigations into corruption in the New South Wales police service, the Wood Commission noted that the code of silence was "essentially a shield against complaint, for example, in circumstances where an officer has stepped out of line in the heat of the moment, but it is equally powerful in those cases where deliberately corrupt practices have been embraced" (Wood, 1997, p. 108). Notably, a 2009 report building on a previous analysis of survey data on police agency integrity found that under certain conditions "police culture fosters corruption" (see Marche, 2009, p. 463; Klockars et al., 2000).

A code of silence can be found in every country, but the conduct officers are willing to protect varies greatly by country (Ivković, 2021; Loyens, 2009; Miller, 2006). Historical, political, social, and economic conditions in a country likely influence the level of police integrity and norms of police behavior.

Correlational evidence presented to the committee by Sanja Kutnjak Ivković (2021) showed that an officer's likelihood of reporting misconduct depended on the perceived severity of the case, assumptions about the likelihood of other officers reporting (i.e., perceived norm), and perceptions that the expected discipline will be fair or too harsh. Wolfe and Piquero (2011) also report that officers who experience fair treatment by their supervisors show less commitment to the code of silence. Further, there is some evidence that other officers reporting misconduct can promote a new organizational culture that is more supportive of reporting (Ivković et al., 2018).

There are also whistleblower mechanisms that allow for individuals to break the code of silence. Whistleblowers play an important role in exposing wrongdoing that threatens public interests, and by protecting them from unfair treatment such as retaliation, discrimination, or disadvantage, individuals may be emboldened to report wrongdoing (Transparency International, 2018). Emerging international standard and practice is to allow whistleblowers to directly report the wrongdoing to competent external authorities, such as independent oversight bodies, anti-corruption commissions, ombudsman institutions (Transparency International, 2018). This practice does remove or replace internal reporting mechanisms, and it is still recommended that employees report internally first. However, legally obliging them to do so may result in complete silence for those who do not feel comfortable reporting internally for various reasons.

The role and influence of supervisors have been framed both positively and negatively in research. In theory, if supervisors take their responsibility seriously and have the resources to monitor, track, mentor, and guide their officers according to the ROL and with the intention of protecting the population, then police use of force may be better controlled. However, there is another view: that in practice, supervisors do not have the resources and cannot devote sufficient attention to effectively monitor and guide their officers. Aggressive supervisors, moreover, may not serve as good role models for controlling uses of force by officers.

Nonetheless, supervisors are generally seen as having significant influence over their officers, whether positively or negatively, by their actions or inactions. Early studies on the role of supervision in police use of force used surveys to correlate officer attitudes and behaviors to supervisors' attitudes and behaviors (Engel, 2000, 2001, 2002; Engel and Worden, 2005). Using these techniques, Engel (2000) identified that officers who were more likely to use force also had supervisors who were more aggressive in the field in that they tended to take over situations or played more of a dual role as both a street officer and a supervisor. We note that these results should be considered correlational, as the assignment process that connected officers to supervisors was unreported.

A more recent study used a RCT research design to examine the impact of procedurally fair supervision on officers' uses of force (Owens et al., 2018). In this study, officers identified as working in high-risk-circumstances were randomly assigned to either a treatment or control condition. In the treatment condition, officers had a non-disciplinary meeting with their supervisor in which the supervisor modeled procedurally fair behavior, reviewed a recent incident the officer engaged in, and pointed out areas of success and potential areas for improvement. This cognitive debrief was juxtaposed to the control group who were subject to only "status quo" supervision. As a result of the intervention, treated officers were less likely than control officers to engage in uses of force in the six weeks following their supervisory meeting. The study by Owens and colleagues (2018) is particularly promising as it not only finds support for the idea that supervisors have a meaningful impact on officers' uses of force but also identifies a specific intervention that can promote this type of supervision in a U.S. city context. The extent to which the findings could generalize to other contexts is unknown, but it points to a promising avenue for future research.

Preparation for supervisors is a needed complement to training efforts. While leading by example and good mentorship are two important components of supervision, providing organizational accountability mechanisms that can support supervision is also key. For example, supervisors need to be empowered to be able to effectively identify, monitor, correct, discipline, track, and report problematic behavior. In its second report on policing training (NASEM, 2022, pp. 29–30), the committee discussed these concepts at length:

Supervisors may need to be trained on how to effectively conduct daily observations and audits of what officers are doing, including training on the right inquiries that will help them determine what officers are doing (NASEM, 2021). They may need training on how to spend their time during the day to effectively balance their administrative duties with observing or auditing officers at the right times and situations. Some assessments of officer performance might also come from analytic sources that supervisors either have to interpret or create. Training on gathering, collating, and analyzing personnel activities or even crime data to better understand officer behavior is critical.

If supervisors are to ensure that officers implement the skills and knowledge they receive in training, the supervisors themselves may also need to be trained in coaching, mentorship, and leadership techniques. This will enable them to relate to, communicate with, and educate officers who either need daily help or more serious remediation for long-term lack of alignment with training. Supervisors may also need to acquire training in accessing and using an agency's accountability infrastructure, assuming that such infrastructure exists, when serious concerns and violations of officer activities occur. For example, supervisors need a clear understanding of the various internal discipline and internal affairs processes that help supervisors correct poor behavior, including how to use those processes. Supervisors may also need training on how body-worn cameras and automatic vehicle locators function with regard to their accountability effects. Again, everyday accountability mechanisms such as performance metrics, inspections, and audits are part of this accountability infrastructure that supervisors need training upon.

In sum, supervisors are influencers within their departments, with results from early studies suggesting that officers' use of force is correlated with the leadership style and activities engaged in by their supervisors (Engel, 2000). More recent results demonstrate short-term reductions in use of force among officers that experienced meetings with supervisors' modeling of procedurally fair behavior and providing reflection and feedback on their interactions with citizens compared to officers without such meetings (i.e., only subjected to the "status quo" supervision) (Owens et al., 2018). These findings reinforce the potential importance of reform efforts that target first-line supervisors, specifically providing them with the resources necessary to carry out effective supervision.

TECHNOLOGICAL INNOVATIONS

Technologies could be used to support effective supervision and also to more directly manage officers. Using technology to monitor officer behavior has gained increasing interest in recent years, especially given that policing is a profession in which supervision is often lacking or not present at all. In its first report (NASEM, 2021), the committee identified several emerging technologies capable of capturing information on police and monitoring officers on the job, including automatic vehicle locators, body-worn cameras, information technologies, and systems for early identification of officers at risk of serious misconduct or suicide. This discussion focuses primarily on body-worn cameras given the larger base of research on the utilization of this technology compared to others and appreciation that findings regarding reductions in use of force may apply to other technologies designed to monitor police behaviors. Of note, the usage of any technology for monitoring police behavior and police–citizen interactions comes with well-founded concerns regarding privacy and civil rights. When considering integrating any form of technology into policing and the ability of officers to leverage technologies such as connected devices and private surveillance systems, agencies should consider expectations of privacy, the impact of surveillance on marginalized communities, and the need for transparency and accountabilty, particularly as technology evolves faster than regulations.

Vehicle cameras and officer-worn/body-worn cameras (BWCs) are an accountability technology that has been rapidly diffusing across police agencies globally. BWCs are small video and audio devices worn by officers on their clothing or glasses, which can be turned on manually or automatically, depending on the policies and rules of agencies and sometimes at the officer's discretion. When turned on, a BWC records interactions and events from the officer's point of view, as cameras are pointed outward from the officer. The reasons and expectations for BWC adoption and use can differ between police and citizens (Lum et al., 2019). In North America, the rapid adoption of BWCs was fueled by citizens' concerns about police use of excessive force and lack of accountability in officer-involved shootings, particularly shootings of Black Americans. Citizens and advocacy groups expect that BWCs will increase the transparency and accountability of the police, especially in their use of force, and deter officer misbehaviors (Ariel et al., 2015; Crow et al., 2017; Culhane et al., 2016; Ellis et al., 2015; President's Task Force on 21st Century Policing, 2015; Sousa et al., 2018). However, several surveys of officers using BWCs indicate that officers like using them because they believe cameras can hold citizens accountable for their criminal activity (Lum et al., 2019).

Although this technology has only become more prevalent in use during the past 10 years, researchers have developed a substantial body of research on BWCs. The two most comprehensive reviews of the literature in this area have been conducted by Lum and colleagues (2019), who reviewed all empirical research on BWCs related to a wide variety of outcomes, and Lum and colleagues (2020), who conducted a Campbell meta-analysis of the most rigorous research on the impacts of BWCs on officer and citizen behavior. These studies have examined evidence from various settings, including small and large agencies within the United States, the United Kingdom, and other countries. These reviews report on BWCs' impacts on several outcomes, but the measured outcomes most relevant to the current discussion are complaints against the police and use of force by officers.

The 2020 meta-analysis conducted by Lum and colleagues suggests that current evidence is insufficient for concluding that BWCs consistently reduce officer use-of-force. On average, officers with cameras, compared to officers without them, experienced a 6.8 percent relative reduction in the use of force incidents across the studies examined. This finding was not statistically significant, and there is substantial uncertainty in this effect. Employing a moderator analysis, Lum and colleagues (2020) suggest that BWCs could be more likely to reduce police use of force if officers' discretion in turning cameras on and off is highly restricted by their agencies (although this idea is still very tentative from the totality of research and does not often reflect reality in BWC use). In other words, a decline in the use of force through BWCs likelyrequires strict enforcement and supervision to ensure that cameras are worn and regularly turned on to discern where use of force would not be clearly proportionate to the event, or only for newer officers.

This meta-analysis also found that officers wearing cameras tend to have lower levels of citizen complaints than officers who are not wearing cameras. However, the research does not indicate whether this decline in complaints reflects a decline in community members' reporting behaviors (they might be less inclined to file minor or unfounded complaints), changes in officer or citizen behaviors toward one another, or improvements in police–community relationships more generally. In other words, it is not clear from the evidence on citizen complaints that BWCs have improved community members' satisfaction with or perceptions of the police, which would be expected if BWCs had a substantial effect on police behavior. Tellingly, surveys of police officers indicate that they do not believe that BWCs will substantially change their behavior (Headley et al., 2017; Pelfrey and Keener, 2016).

Further research on BWCs continues to accumulate, and now includes two evaluations in South America. A recent RCT of officers in Santa Catarina, Brazil, conducted by Barbosa and colleagues (2021), found that BWCs can lead to less use of force and improved interactions between people and police, particularly for dispatched events that are lower in seriousness and for those events involving more junior-level officers. Using a "negative interaction index" that combined charges of contempt, disobedience, resistance, and use of handcuffs or arrests (developed by Anderson, 2008), Barbosa and colleagues also found that police dispatches that involved BWCs had significant declines in these negative interactions.

Again, these findings were most likely for less-serious events and with more junior officers. In Uruguay, Mitchell and colleagues (2018) examined the impact of BWCs using a combination of BWCs and procedural justice scripts that officers used when stopping individuals for traffic offenses. This study indicated that complaints declined for officers with BWCs, although the data were unable to disentangle the impact of BWCs from the procedural justice scripts.

Further concerns have been raised regarding the implementation of BWCs. In many locations across the United States, the cost of BWCs remains the primary concern, with agencies having to account not only for the cost of the cameras themselves, but also video storage and disposal, and ongoing maintenance (Van Ness, 2020). There are also no established, uniform international standards for the implementation and use of BWCs, leaving a patchwork of policies that may result in a loss of the potential positive benefits of using BWCs. While the International Association of Chiefs of Police released model policy in 2014 on the purpose (IACP, 2014), policy, and procedures around BWCs, the lack of uniform standards and regulations raises questions regarding the discretionary power given to officers in operating the camera, and the potential for invasion of privacy.

Overall, BWCs have real potential to curb the most egregious behaviors of police violence, and as the most recent study in Brazil indicates, they may curb excessive force in lower-seriousness events that may not warrant the use of force. However, given the totality of the research evidence, the anticipated effects of BWCs as an accountability technology for policing may have been overestimated. This is consistent with the mixed, modest, and sometimes unintended effects that technologies have more generally in policing and with the fact that the impact of technology depends on agency infrastructure and functioning. Like other technologies, the effectiveness of BWCs depends on how they are used, who uses them, and how their use is monitored and supervised. These mediating factors depend on the will of the agency to implement several accountability mechanisms that could affect these factors. Mechanisms such as effective training in the use of these technologies from the outset, external monitoring bodies, and administrative policies and interventions to disincentivize the use of force are all possible tools that may be coupled with the implementation of technology to create a more effective plan for meeting the goal of reducing police use of force.

ADMINISTRATIVE INCENTIVES

This category includes policies and interventions administered internally to discourage use of force across the entire police agency. Though there are many types of administrative measures, this section focuses on promising approaches carried out in Brazil as reported in Cano (2021). The unifying element of these initiatives is that they change the benefits, or costs, that officers may associate with using force.

Initiatives to Monitor Police Use of Force by Institution and Unit

These initiatives were generally designed to bring down lethality and improve internal control but also serve to potentially raise awareness that an officer's actions are being recorded and observed by their supervisors and the public. The simple fact that force is being monitored can send a signal that deaths in the course of police work should be limited. For example, in the State of São Paulo, Brazil, a Special Commission for the Reduction of Lethality in Actions involving Police Officers (Comissão Especial Para Redução da Letalidade em Ações Envolvendo Policiais) was created in 2000 (Cano, 2021). This commission was tasked with reviewing incident reports from police officers involved in shootouts to identify risk factors and with proposing preventive measures to reduce deaths in police encounters. There are no known evaluations of the impact of this commission. The State of Minas Gerais, also in Brazil, published an annual report on the use of lethal force for a number of years starting in 2005. These reports ranked police units according to the number of people killed by their officers in an effort to increase transparency and create pressure on commanders to reduce their officers' use of force or otherwise justify the fatal interactions (Cano, 2021).

Initiatives to Monitor Police Use of Force by Individual Officer

Initiatives to monitor individual officers' use of force may be helpful for establishing patterns among units and discovering which officers may need to be retrained, or even disciplined. Where data exist, trends tend to show that incidents of lethal force are concentrated among specific units and particular officers (Cano, 2021). In 2014, the Military Police of Rio de Janeiro asked the State University of Rio to create an index to help identify officers at risk of using force excessively (Osse and Cano, 2017). The index measured individual officers' consumption of ammunition during the previous six months, weighting it by the prevailing level of violence in the area of his or her beat and by the type of function the officer performed (on-foot patrolling, car patrolling, tactical response, etc.). Those who exceeded the expected average by more than two standard deviations were chosen for retraining. The program was introduced experimentally but later discontinued. It was not submitted to evaluation.

Economic Incentives

Several Brazilian states have resorted to economic incentives to try to bring crime rates down. In 2009, the state of Rio de Janeiro created the Integrated System of Targets and Results Monitoring (Sistema Integrado de Metas e Acompanhamentos de Resultados—SIM) (Estado do Rio de Janeiro, Brasil, 2009). Under this system, police units receive pay bonuses according to homicide and robbery rates in their area, with the reduction of the former having more weight. An indicator called "violent lethality" was added in 2011 and included the number of civilians killed in police interventions together with recorded homicides (Cano, 2021). Police units who used lethal force more often reduced their likelihood of receiving a bonus. This policy change was just one of several taking place in Rio de Janeiro at the time. It is unclear whether this policy, another policy, or the whole set of policy changes had the greatest influence on the decline in the number of persons killed by police. Nonetheless, in 2011, 2012, and 2013, this metric reached its lowest points in many years: 523, 414, and 413 deaths, respectively (a roughly 50 percent drop from 2009, when police killed 1,048 civilians) (Cano, 2021).

CONCLUSION

As this chapter makes clear, there are sizeable gaps in our knowledge of the efficacy of use of force interventions, but several promising approaches warrant further implementation, testing, and evaluation. As required by an evidence-based approach to policing, the committee emphasizes that the promising approaches outlined above, when implemented, must be evaluated with attention to systematically measuring field outcomes across time (short, medium, and long term), and when possible—across space. These approaches need to be continuously assessed to determine what conditions are optimal, and the context in which certain measures work well, do not work, or have unintended consequences.

3

Committee's Conclusions and Recommendations

Recent events around the globe, such as the killing of George Floyd by a police officer in the United States, the abuses of Nigeria's Special Anti-Robbery Squad, violent repression of protests in Colombia, and unprecedented numbers of police killings in Rio de Janeiro have piqued public concern about police use-of-force practices, policies, and controls. Injury and death from use of excessive force by police officers in the task of upholding the rule of law (ROL) and other objectives of the state have been viewed by many as human rights violations. Thus, the committee was asked to examine the policies and practices for police use of force that effectively promote the ROL and protect the population in the international context.

Protecting human rights in the course of policing need not be an obstacle to reducing crime. Rather, the protection of human rights is foundational for promoting the ROL and fairness in the application of the law. Unfortunately, research has shown that communities and populations, particularly (but not exclusively) in the Global South,[1] often see agressive use of force by police as a necessity to reduce the level of violence and control criminals (Americas Barometer, 2019; Bailey et al., 2013; Flores-Macias and Zarkin, 2021). This perceived public support can be used to justify encouraging a scale of force that may lead to an increase of police encounters with killings of citizens, continued violence, as well as severe restrictions on appropriate justice and community safety.

---

[1] The committee uses the term "Global South" to refer to low- to middle-income countries most likely to receive assistance from the Bureau of International Narcotics and Law Enforcement Affairs (INL). "Global North" refers to developed countries, notably the United States and the United Kingdom, and includes Australia despite its geographic location.

Efforts to incorporate human rights principles into police reforms have been challenging. Research studies have observed real backlash and other unintended consequences of such attempts, including increased vigilantism and extrajudicial violence (Hanson and Kronick, forthcoming). Such concerning outcomes suggest that interventions aimed at minimizing police use of force may need to be accompanied by the adoption of evidence-based strategies to promote crime reduction. This may be particularly true where aggressive and even indiscriminate displays of force have historically been central to police operations.

Historical reviews of police reforms indicate that a multipronged approach, with mechanisms both internal and external to police agencies, are promising. The committee encourages consideration and implementation of nested layers of policies, practices, and accountability mechanisms for tracking, monitoring, and disciplining police use of force, and training officers on when to use force legally and how to do so with great constraint. Given the current state of global policing and the variations in how physical force and weapons are used in different contexts, in many respects reform efforts are going to be "building the airplane as it is flying." While there are notable differences across contexts, several countries seem to have similarities, including gaps in record-keeping, policy compliance, and supervision and accountability infrastructure. As such, data collection is critical to track progress, measure outcomes, and support rigorous research efforts.

In this chapter, the committee calls attention to multiple elements that, if supported by international donor organizations, would improve the knowledge available on incidents of use of excessive force and their prevention. These include guidance for improving the tracking, monitoring, and supervision of officer use of force and identifying effective interventions aimed at reducing police use of force. This chapter highlights the committee's significant findings (observations based on facts and research results), conclusions (expert judgments about the findings), and recommendations (calls for action or change) regarding data collection and use-of-force policies, training, oversight, and supervision.

DATA NEEDS

The current state of research on police use of force is crippled by a lack of reliable tracking and data collected on even lethal uses of force, let alone nonlethal force. Diverse definitions of "excessive" force, as well as the wide range of injuries and rights violations, create complexities that few nations have been able to track with precision. Even a reliable, official annual count of people killed in police interactions is generally unavailable across the Global South. Notably, standardized national data on police use of force are also absent in the United States (Shane, 2018). One of the most critical government actions required to control the use of force is to develop, resource, and institutionalize a reliable, transparent, and consistent system of recording civilian deaths by police. Failure to do so creates a prima facie threat to the ROL.

> **FINDING:** Currently available data on police use of force are generally insufficient to understand the nature and extent of police use of force. Lack of reliable data hampers the ability to evaluate the effectiveness of practices designed to reduce police use of force.

Establishing good practices for ongoing and systematic measurement is essential to provide the necessary information for public policy, to identify and control problem areas before they reach crisis levels, and to achieve continuous improvements. The same can be said about establishing a measurement system to restore a failing institution; it enables the identification of problems and potential solutions. The quality and reliability of recorded data are critical, and with a plan in place and the appropriate allocation of resources, data collection is not a significant burden on officers or institutions. While the need for measurement is recognized across the police and justice reform communities, developing specific measurements that are relevant, collectible, and elucidating is a significant challenge. In addition to commonly collected data such as training outcomes, periodic comparison of official records to independently generated estimates should be part of a measurement system. For example, journalistic accounts can potentially identify under- (or over-) reporting in official records. This has been the case in the United States, where the *Washington Post*, for the last six years, has counted every fatal shooting by an on-duty police officer in the country through crowdsourced information derived from news accounts, social media posts, and police reports (Tate et al., 2022).

> **RECOMMENDATION 1:** Significant gaps in measurement related to police use of force exist. International donor organizations, such as INL, should support local and/or national systems in the collection and dissemination of standardized information about use of force by law enforcement officers. Priority should be given to the documentation and publication by an independent medical examiner or coroner of every case where someone (citizen or police) dies as a result of a police encounter. Where these systems do not function reliably, donors should strongly support their creation or efforts to improve them.

Through funding mechanisms, international donor organizations are uniquely positioned to encourage implementing partners to collect standardized information about force used by officers in the field. This type of data collection could occur within existing police reform programs, or it could be accomplished as a new program designed to test strategies to collect accurate data. In addition to clarifying the physical aspects of force (e.g., the discharge of a firearm, physical attack with a close-fisted strike, etc.), data collection needs to be sufficient to estimate the likelihood that any force used was proportional to a reasonable assessment of the immediate threat.

> **CONCLUSION:** The development of a measurement system and appropriate data collection is complex and context-specific. An assessment of a country's legal framework will be necessary to determine current laws and gaps in laws governing police use of force. Such an assessment will help define excessive force and benchmarks to hold officers accountable for a given context.

> **RECOMMENDATION 2:** While most use of force by police is not lethal, frequent incidences of excessive force can cause great harm to the public and undermine the ROL and trust in the police, and in the state institutions more broadly. International donor organizations such as INL should encourage and fund police agencies to develop and enforce digital record-keeping on each use of force incident with or with potential of serious injuries, such as all police–citizen interactions where firearms or other weapons are employed. These records should identify officers using force, the nature of force and weapon used, the locations of the incidents, the time and date of each incident, as well as personal identifiers and demographic information for citizens involved. Technical assistance should be granted to develop ongoing analyses of the patterns of less-than-lethal-force incidents, including concentrations of events among individual officers, specific places and times.

This standardized data collection is necessary for tracking the progress of reform efforts and having the information necessary to make adjustments. It is also necessary to further develop an evidence base from which a scientific consensus can be built, concerning how policy or training can reduce the frequency of force that degrades the ROL.

> **RECOMMENDATION 3:** Innovations intended to minimize police use of force should be supported by international donor organizations, such as INL. Police agencies should work in partnerships with independent social and data scientists to design impact assessments in order to evaluate and continuously improve their reform programs.

The sufficiency of data collection and analysis is best determined by researchers with expertise in multiple ways of capturing data on police–citizen interactions and in rigorous approaches to collecting, recording, and analyzing the data. International donor organizations could consider including this stipulation to work with scientists on data collection and impact assessments in contracts, grants, and agreements.

One example of how the necessary data could be constructed, in a way that is both informative from a scientific perspective and less likely to impose an undue burden on law enforcement agencies, would be to include a checklist of types of physical engagement used by an officer, as well as the behavior and posed threats of the citizens involved, that could be filled out in conjunction with the reporting of an arrest. While this would not capture the universe of all force used, such a requirement adds a small amount of paperwork to what is (in many cases) an existing form most officers complete, rather than the creation of an entirely new administrative task for the officer. This also would allow for a linkage between the type and frequency of force used by type of crime, allowing for an assessment of proportionality.

Finally, the committee notes that there is some evidence (a pre-post comparison) from Sao Paulo and Dallas that instructing officers to collect data on force, and using the frequency of force used by all officers in a division as an internal metric to evaluate command staff, may itself be an effective strategy to reduce police violence (Cano, 2021). The need to fill in a detailed report has, in some cases, served as a warning that use of force is meant to be an exceptional measure and subject to scrutiny.

In an ideal world, every incident when a police officer uses force, however minor, could be recorded and analyzed. However, it can be difficult to achieve this goal without dedicated resources and effort, even in the context of developed democracies. The committee has developed a shortlist of priority data: counts of people (both civilians and police) who die during police encounters; counts of people shot (both citizens and police) in police encounters; and counts of deaths in police custody. These counts should be supplemented with data on demographics of persons killed or injured, nature of crime or disorder for the police intervention, time of day, location, and nature of death or injury.[2] While it is possible to measure other things, nothing is more important than the number of people who die during police encounters.

In developing a data infrastructure, stakeholders need to consider who and what institutions will be involved in collecting and verifying the data and ensuring quality control. Appropriate incentive structures are also

---

[2] See Dallas Police Department website for an example of publicly reported data for on-duty officer involved shootings (https://dallaspolice.net/ois/ois). The Police Data Initiative also catalogues available use of force datasets for agencies in the United States (https://www.policedatainitiative.org/datasets/use-of-force/).

important to encourage accurate data collection. Unintended consequences need to be considered, particularly when incentives (e.g., bonuses, promotions) encourage false reporting. Multiple independent systems for collecting and publishing data on police use of force can serve as checks for other systems. For example, in the United States, the Centers for Disease Control and Prevention (CDC) maintains the National Violent Death Reporting System, which tracks data including fatalities resulting from the use of force by officers on duty. A 2016 comparison found that the National Violent Death Reporting System provides more complete data on deaths in police encounters than existing systems, such as the Federal Bureau of Investigation's Supplementary Homicide Reports, the CDC's National Vital Statistics System, and the Bureau of Justice Statistics Arrest-Related Deaths Program, all of which have issues with serious underreporting of these deaths (Barber et al., 2016; Loftin et al., 2003; Shields and Ward, 2008).

As discussed in the committee's second report (NASEM, 2022), to report data accurately, police officers will need the skills to understand basic crime information and trends and appreciate how the data collected and analyzed can be used to improve policing operations, safeguard their role as guardians, and protect the communities they serve.

The committee recognizes that capabilities and resources will vary across different countries. For example, some police stations are without computers or even electricity. While many places will have in-house tools and resources, or be able to leverage the Internet for crowdsourced information, some places will have to launch their data infrastructure with rudimentary tools. In either case, the goal is the same: to develop a measurement system to routinely and accurately count incidents to effectively measure and manage police use of force. There are likely various methods of counting fatalities by police across and within countries. A comparison of methods across countries in the Global South could be conducted to determine the extent to which there are multiple ways of measuring people killed by the police, how they compare, and which methods—of collection and verification—lead to more consistent counts.

USE OF FORCE POLICIES

Given the information presented to it, the committee finds that laws and policies on police use of force in many countries fall short of incorporating tenets of international human rights standards (Flores, 2021). There is much room for improvement in translating international human rights standards to national laws and police policies at the organizational level. This is true in both the Global North and the Global South. However, we recognize that legal or policy compliance with international standards is neither necessary nor sufficient for police actions to be consistent with the

ROL. Nonetheless, they can serve as powerful frameworks to guide police reform and use of force policies and practices.

In almost all policing contexts, police have written directives from the government and/or agency itself on when, how, and under what circumstances lethal force can be used. From the studies and cases shared at the workshop, the committee determined that use of force policies serve three critical purposes:

1. *Informative*: Policies provide a mechanism for educating and re-educating police officers on what is directed and permissible under law and what are the expected considerations for deciding whether a use of force is appropriate. Having clear, documented policies on use of force can increase the likelihood that officers have accurate information about when force is appropriate and lawful
2. *Administrative*: Policies can disincentivize the use of force, through both carrots and sticks, particularly the use of force that exceeds the minimum amount necessary to establish control over a situation.
3. *Restrictive*: Policies can prohibit the use of force in certain situations (e.g., curbing shots on fleeing suspects who pose no threat to other individuals).

Policies on police use of force are an important part of layered efforts to reduce the occurrence of excessive force. It is fundamental to promoting the ROL and protecting the population to have policies that are clear, impartially enforced, aligned to local laws and international human rights standards, inclusive of mechanisms for civilian oversight, and regularly communicated to police officers through ongoing training opportunities.

> **RECOMMENDATION 4:** International donor organizations, such as INL, should work with implementing partners to ensure that policies on police use of force have been developed or reviewed in consultation with relevant police oversight bodies and ombuds institutions. These policies should be impartially enforced, clearly defined, aligned with human rights standards, inclusive of mechanisms for civilian oversight, communicated to police officers through ongoing training opportunities, and regularly reviewed for effectiveness.

TRAINING FOR POLICE OFFICERS

It almost goes without saying that training (both formal and informal, both in classroom and on the job) is a critical component of efforts to control and restrain police use of force. However, open questions revolve around what content should be delivered, how, and with what frequency. In its second report (NASEM, 2022), the committee offered that incorporating empirical facts about and well-accepted theories of crime and victimization into training can provide the foundational knowledge police officers need to make more informed decisions about managing crime, offenders, and victims. The committee concludes that these facts and theories not only form the building blocks of police strategies that are now known to be effective at reducing crime but can also inform policies, strategies, and everyday police actions that better protect the public from harm.

Research is just beginning to examine the consequences (positive or negative) of training designed for other purposes on police use of force. Much existing research regarding use of force has focused on training that was specifically aimed at reducing use of force that might be excessive, often in response to significant events of police misconduct and public complaints. This type of training has centered on developing procedural justice and de-escalation skills, and/or educating officers on human rights documents and principles. Other trainings have focused on how to use force in a non-lethal manner.

> **FINDING:** Evaluations of police training, with few exceptions, have been limited to measuring officers' attitudes, opinions, and knowledge before and after the training and/or officer performance in simulated exercises. Police training programs have not been sufficiently evaluated in ways to verify their effectiveness in changing officer behaviors (such as their use of force) in the field (on the job).

Although such evaluations of attitudes are relevant, it is not known whether the expression of different attitudes by police officers, in a context where social desirability may lead them to do so, ultimately affects the way they behave in the field. Numerous scholars have noted that informal socialization and police (sub)cultures are at least as important as formal training in determining police behavior, including with respect to the use of force (Belur, 2010; Chan, 2000). This issue also has been noted previously by the National Academies (NASEM, 2018). The continued resistance of policing agencies to linking training and officer actions is detrimental to improving practice and building credible police science.

> **RECOMMENDATION 5:** International donor organizations should incentivize robust evaluations of training outcomes through extra funding assistance for partners willing to evaluate training programs, particularly any programs aimed at improving officers' skills at de-escalating situations before resorting to use of force. Where possible, evaluations should be done by comparing on-the-job actions taken by training participants and non-participants and linking completion

of these programs with official records and data on use of force over time.

Ideally, impact evaluation of such training would monitor incidents of use of force by officers over time to compare the results among those who took the training with the results among those who did not. Such evaluations can be expensive and time-consuming and require the full cooperation of the law enforcement institution involved. That said, dedicating more time and resources to this critical topic is a vital first step in reducing the use of excessive force.

Moreover, studies that attempt to replicate existing evaluations of police training are needed, as the existing evidence base for any particular training programs is limited to studies of individual jurisdictions. Replication is important for knowledge accumulation and to improve confidence in the generalizability of the findings. Further, most existing evaluations of training programs have evaluated those that involve one or two days of training. Best practices for adult learning in training from other fields suggest that high-repetition training over more prolonged periods is important for both retention and understanding (Ericsson, 2004; Ericsson and Ward, 2007).

OVERSIGHT AND SUPERVISION

Chapter 2 discussed different accountability measures to monitor and restrain police use of force: external oversight bodies, internal control mechanisms, technological innovations to prevent abuses of power, and administrative incentives. The committee views accountability systems as critical to the control of police use of force. It recognizes that contextual factors will affect the success of accountability measures and encourages continuous, systematic assessment across time to track outcomes and unintended consequences and adjust policies and practices as warranted. It also supports mechanisms to engage the public in providing oversight to police use of force. Members of the public need to be able to report and file complaints against officers or entire agencies, preferably to an independent investigating body (NASEM, 2021).

Controlling the use of force requires not only normative approaches through law and guidelines, but mechanisms that support the implementation of use-of-force policies, practices, and normative ideals. While regular reports and information collected through technologies may assist in recording and monitoring uses of force, these systems need layers of active supervision that not only mentor officers and aim to correct poor behavior, but also track, report, and provide discipline to officers who violate norms, laws, policies, procedures, and training. As discussed in the committee's second report (NASEM, 2022), direct supervisors need training, resources, and institutional support to achieve these goals.

External mechanisms or oversight boards have been instituted or considered in many countries to address deficiencies with internal investigations and discipline and to improve public transparency. There is much variation in how such boards operate, and many studies attribute any shortcomings to the lack of proper investigatory powers, political support, human and financial resources, powers of recommendation and follow-up, and financial and operational independence separate from police and government officials required to carry out truly effective oversight. There is not yet a body of empirical evidence to support the effectiveness of external monitoring bodies to minimize police use of force.

References

African Policing Civilian Oversight Forum (APCOF). (2017). APCOF Annual Report, 2017. *African Policing Civilian Oversight Forum.* http://apcof.org/wp-content/uploads/apcof_annual_report_2017.pdf.

Ahnen, R.E. (2007). The Politics of Police Violence in Democratic Brazil. *Latin American Politics & Society*, 49(1), 141–164.

Alpert, G.P., McLean, K., and Stoughton, S. (2021). *Evidence and Police use of Force: Theories without Data*. Report to the Committee on the Evidence to Advance Reform in the Global Security and Justice Sectors, National Academies of Sciences, Engineering, and Medicine, October 20, 2021. https://www.nationalacademies.org/event/08-26-2021/evidence-to-advance-reform-in-the-global-security-and-justice-sectors-workshop-3-public-session-1.

Americas Barometer. (2019). Vanderbilt University's Latin America Public Opinion Project. https://www.vanderbilt.edu/lapop/raw-data.php.

Amnesty International. (2015). Use of Force: Guidelines for Implementation of the UN Basic Principles on the Use for Force and Firearms by Law Enforcement Officials. Amnesty International. https://www.amnestyusa.org/wp-content/uploads/2017/04/amnesty_international_guidelines_on_use_of_force-2.pdf.

Amnesty International. (2020a). *Iran: At Least 23 Children Killed by Security Forces in November Protests—New Evidence*. Amnesty International. https://www.amnesty.org/en/latest/news/2020/03/iran-at-least-23-children-killed-by-security-forces-in-november-protests-new-evidence/.

Amnesty International. (2020b). *Police Violence around the World*. Amnesty International. https://www.amnestyusa.org/issues/deadly-force-police-accountability-police-violence/.

Amnesty International. (2021). *Police Violence*. Amnesty International. https://www.amnesty.org/en/what-we-do/police-brutality/.

Anderson, M.L. (2008). Multiple inference and gender differences in the effects of early intervention: A reevaluation of the Abecedarian, Perry Preschool, and Early Training projects. *Journal of the American Statistical Association*, 103(484), 1481–1495. https://doi.org/10.1198/016214508000000841.

Ang, D., Bencsik, P., Bruhn, J., and Derenoncourt, E. (2021). Police violence reduces civilian cooperation and engagement with law enforcement. Bravo Working Paper # 2021-005. https://economics.brown.edu/sites/g/files/dprerj726/files/papers/Bravo%20Working%20 Paper%202021-005.pdf.

Ariel, B., Farrar, W.A., and Sutherland, A. (2015). The effect of police body-worn cameras on use of force and citizens' complaints against the police: A randomized controlled trial. *Journal of Quantitative Criminology, 31*(3), 509–535. https://doi.org/10.1007/ s10940-014-9236-3.

Ba, B., Knox, D., Mummolo, J., and Rivera, R. (2021). The Role of Officer Race and Gender in Police-Civilian Interactions in Chicago. *Science, 371*(6530), 696–702.

Barber, C., Azrael, D., Cohen, A., Miller, M., Thymes, D., Wang, D.E., and Hemenway, D. (2016). Homicides by Police: Comparing Counts From the National Violent Death Reporting System, Vital Statistics, and Supplementary Homicide Reports. *American Journal of Public Health, 106*(5), 922–927. https://doi.org/10.2105/AJPH.2016.303074.

Barbosa, D.A.C., Fetzer, T., Soto, C., and Souza, P.C.L. (2021). *De-Escalation Technology: The Impact of Body-Worn Cameras on Citizen-Police Interactions.* CAGE Research Centre, University of Warwick. https://warwick.ac.uk/fac/soc/economics/research/centres/cage/ publications/workingpapers/2021/de_escalation_technology_the_impact_of_body_worn_ cameras_on_citizen_police_interactions/.

Bailey, J., Paras, P., and Vargas, D. (2013). "¿El ejército como policía? Correlación de la confianza pública en la policía, el sistema judicial, y los militares," *Política y Gobierno,* 161-185.

Bayley, D.H. (1985). *Patterns of Policing: A Comparative International Policing.* New Brunswick, NJ: Rutgers University Press.

BBC. (2020a). Hong Kong protests: Police tackle 12-year-old girl to the ground. September 7. https://www.bbc.com/news/world-asia-china-54056356.

BBC. (2020b). Rio violence: Police killings reach record high in 2019. January 23. https:// www.bbc.com/news/world-latin-america-51220364.

Belur, J. (2010). *Permission to Shoot?: Police Use of Deadly Force in Democracies.* Springer Science & Business Media. https://link.springer.com/book/10.1007/978-1-4419-0975-6.

Benedek, W. (2018). *Organization for Security and Co-operation in Europe Rapporteur's Report under the Moscow Mechanism on Alleged Human Rights Violations and Impunity in the Chechen Republic of the Russian Federation.* Office for Democratic Institutions and Human Rights. https://www.osce.org/files/Moscow%20Mechanism%20 Document_ENG.pdf.

Biernert, A., Maloney, M., and Masters, S. (2015). *Use of Force: Guidelines for Implementation of the UN Basic Principles on the Use of Force and Firearms by Law Enforcement Officials.* Amnesty International. https://www.amnestyusa.org/files/amnesty_international_ guidelines_on_use_of_force-2.pdf.

Bingham, T. (2011). *The Rule of Law.* Penguin UK.

Blair, G. Weinstein, J.M., Christia, F., Arias, E., Badran, E., Blair, R., Cheema, A., Farooqui, A., Fetzer, T., Grossman, G., Haim, D., Hameed, Z., Hanson, R. Hasanain, A., Kronick, D., Morse, B., Muggah, R., Nadeem, F., Tsai, L., Nanes, M., Slough, T., Ravanilla, N., Shapiro, J., Silva, B., Souza, P., and Wilke, A. (2021). Community policing does not build citizen trust in police or reduce crime in the Global South. *Science, 374*(6571), eabd3446. https://doi.org/10.1126/science.abd3446.

Bottoms, A.E., and Tankebe, J. (2017). *Police Legitimacy and the Authority of the State.* Hart Publishing Limited.

Bruce, D. (2020). How to reduce police brutality in South Africa. *Institute for Security Studies, Southern Africa Report, 40,* 1–20. https://journals.co.za/doi/abs/10.10520/ejc- issar-v2020-n40-a1.

Bullock, J. (2021). Why Limiting Police Use of Lethal Force Led to Broad Decreases in Violence in Rio de Janeiro. Presentation Prepared for the Harvard Political Economy Workshop on February 2, 2021. https://web.lists.fas.harvard.edu/archive/list/gov3007-l @lists.fas.harvard.edu/message/WM54MCCMK6BULVEIOLC4GC7NKHTUKCVJ/ attachment/4/Bullock_PE_Workshop.pdf.

Cano, I. (2021). *Policies and Practices to Control Police Use of Force in the "Global South."* Paper prepared for the Committee on the Evidence to Advance Reform in the Global Security and Justice Sectors, National Academies of Sciences, Engineering, and Medicine. https://www.nationalacademies.org/event/08-26-2021/evidence-to-advance-reform-in-the-global-security-and-justice-sectors-workshop-3-public-session-1.

Chan, J.B. (2000). Backstage punishment: Police violence, occupational culture and criminal justice. *Violence and Police Culture, Melbourne*, 85–108. https://doi.org/10.1080/10345329.2001.12036231.

Chanin, J. (2015). Examining the sustainability of pattern or practice police misconduct reform. *Police Quarterly 18*, 163–192.

Chanin, J. (2017). Police Reform Through an Administrative Lens: Revisiting the Justice Department's Pattern or Practice Initiative. *Administrative Theory & Praxis, 39*(4), 257–274. https://doi.org/10.1080/10841806.2017.1381479.

Cheung, A.Y. (2019). *Measuring the Measures: Rule of Law Indices and Abusive Legalism*. https://doi.org/10.31228/osf.io/8r5zb.

Chillar, V.F. (2021). The racial divide at micro places: A pre/post analysis of the effects of the Newark Consent Decree on field inquiries (2015–2017). *Journal of Research in Crime and Delinquency*. https://doi.org/10.1177/00224278211030964.

Council on Criminal Justice. (2021). Task Force on Policing. Council on Criminal Justice. https://counciloncj.org/tfp/.

Crow, M.S., Snyder, J.A., Crichlow, V.J., and Smykla, J.O. (2017). Community perceptions of police body-worn cameras: The impact of views on fairness, fear, performance, and privacy. *Criminal Justice and Behavior, 44*(4), 589–610. https://doi.org/10.1177/0093854816688037.

Cruz, J.M. (2015). Police Misconduct and Political Legitimacy in Central America. *Journal of Latin American Studies, 47*(2), 251–283.

Culhane, S.E., Boman, J.H., and Schweitzer, K. (2016). Public Perceptions of the Justifiability of Police Shootings: The Role of Body Cameras in a Pre- and Post-Ferguson Experiment. *Police Quarterly, 19*(3), 251–274. https://doi.org/10.1177/1098611116651403.

Curtice, T. (2021). How Repression Affects Public Perceptions of Police: Evidence from a Natural Experiment in Uganda. *Journal of Conflict Resolution, 65*(10), 1680–1780.

Dell, M. (2015). Trafficking Networks and the Mexican Drug War. *American Economic Review, 105*(6), 1738–1779. https://doi.org/10.1257/aer.20121637.

Desmond, M., Papachistos, A.V., Kirk, D.S. (2016). Police Violence and Citizen Crime Reporting in the Black Community. *American Sociological Review, 81*(5), 857–876. https://doi.org/10.1177/0003122416663494.

Ellis, T., Jenkins, C. and Smith, P. (2015). *Evaluation of the Introduction of Personal Issue Body Worn Video Cameras (Operation Hyperion) on the Isle of Wight: Final Report to Hampshire Police, 2015*. University of Portsmouth. http://www.hampshire.police.uk/internet/news-and-appeals/2015/march/05032015-body-worn-video.

Engel, R.S. (2000). The effects of supervisory styles on patrol officer behavior. *Police Quarterly, 3*, 262–293. https://doi.org/10.1177/1098611100003003003.

Engel, R.S. (2001). Supervisory styles of patrol sergeants and lieutenants. *Journal of Criminal Justice, 29*, 341–355.

Engel, R.S. (2002). Patrol officer supervision in the community policing era. *Journal of Criminal Justice, 30*, 51–64. https://doi.org/10.1016/S0047-2352(01)00122-2.

Engel, R.S., Corsaro, N., Isaza, G.T., and McManus, H.D. (2022). Assessing the impact of de-escalation training on police behavior: Reducing police use of force in the Louisville, KY Metro Police Department. *Criminology & Public Policy, Early View.* https://doi.org/10.1111/1745-9133.12574.

Engel, R.S., McManus, H.D., and Herold, T.D. (2017). *The Deafening Demand for De-escalation Training: A Systematic Review and Call for Evidence in Police Use of Force Reform.* International Association of Chiefs of Police. https://www.theiacp.org/sites/default/files/IACP_UC_De-escalation%20Systematic%20Review.pdf.

Engel, R.S., and Worden, R.E. (2006). Police officers' attitudes, behavior, and supervisory influences: An analysis of problem solving. *Criminology, 41*, 131–166. https://doi.org/10.1111/j.1745-9125.2003.tb00984.x.

Ericsson, K.A. (2004). Deliberate practice and the acquisition and maintenance of expert performance in medicine and related domains. *Academic Medicine, 79*(10 Suppl), S70–S81. https://doi.org/10.1097/00001888-200410001-00022.

Ericsson, K.A., and Ward, P. (2007). Capturing the naturally occurring superior performance of experts in the laboratory: Toward a science of expert and exceptional performance. *Current Directions in Psychological Science, 16*, 346–350. https://doi.org/10.1111/j.1467-8721.2007.00533.x.

Espinoza, D. (2021). Presentation to the Committee on the Evidence to Advance Reform in the Global Security and Justice Sectors, National Academies of Sciences, Engineering, and Medicine, October 22, 2021. https://www.nationalacademies.org/event/08-27-2021/evidence-to-advance-reform-in-the-global-security-and-justice-sectors-workshop-3-public-session-2.

Estado do Rio de Janeiro, Brazil (2009). *Decreto n. 41931/2009. Dispõe Sobre O Sistema De Definição E Gerenciamento De Metas Para Os Indicadores Estratégicos De Criminalidade Do Estado Do Rio De Janeiro E Dá Outras Providências.* Rio de Janeiro. https://biblioteca.pge.rj.gov.br/scripts/bnweb/bnmapi.exe?router=upload/27425.

European Court of Human Rights. (2021). *European Convention on Human Rights.* Council of Europe. https://www.echr.coe.int/documents/convention_eng.pdf.

Evans, W.N. and Owens, E.G. (2007). COPS and crime. *Journal of Public Economics. Elsevier. 91*(1-2), 181–201. https://doi.org/10.1016/j.jpubeco.2006.05.014.

Flores, C. (2021). Presentation to the Committee on the Evidence to Advance Reform in the Global Security and Justice Sectors, National Academies of Sciences, Engineering, and Medicine, October 20, 2021. https://www.nationalacademies.org/event/08-27-2021/evidence-to-advance-reform-in-the-global-security-and-justice-sectors-workshop-3-public-session-2.

Flores-Macias, G. and Zarkin, J. (2021). Militarization and Perceptions of Law Enforcement in the Developing World: Evidence from a Conjoint Experiment in Mexico. *British Journal of Political Science*, 1–21. https://doi.org/10.1017/S0007123421000259.

Gandhi, D., Heyns, C., Maslen, S., Orao, B., Oyakhirome, I.L., Probert, T., Adang, O., Paepe, J.D., Easton, M., Dymond, A., Rappert, B., and Skinner, S. (2021). *Toward a Lethal Force Monitor.* https://lethal-force-monitor.org/downloads/toward-lethal-force-monitor.pdf.

Gingerich, D.W., and Oliveros, V. (2018). Police Violence and the Underreporting of Crime. *Economics & Politics, 30*(1), 78–105. http://doi.wiley.com/10.1111/ecpo.12102.

Goh, L.S. (2020). Going local: Do consent decrees and other forms of federal intervention in municipal police departments reduce police killings? *Justice Quarterly, 37*, 900–929. https://doi.org/10.1080/07418825.2020.1733637.

Goh, L.S. (2021). Did de-escalation successfully reduce serious use of force in Camden County, New Jersey? A synthetic control analysis of force outcomes. *Criminology and Public Policy, 20*, 207–241. https://doi.org/10.1111/1745-9133.12536.

González, Y. (2020). *Authoritarian Police in Democracy: Contested Security in Latin America*. Cambridge University Press.

Hanson, R., and Kronick, D. (forthcoming). Police vigilantism.

Harmon, R. (2009). Promoting civil rights through proactive policing reform. *Stanford Law Review*, 62, 1–68. https://www.stanfordlawreview.org/print/article/promoting-civil-rights-through-proactive-policing-reform/.

Headley, A.M., Guerette, R.T., and Shariati, A. (2017). A field experiment of the impact of body-worn cameras (BWCs) on police officer behavior and perceptions. *Journal of Criminal Justice*, 53(C), 102–109.

Holland, A. (2013). Right on Crime?: Conservative Party Politics and Mano Dura Policies in El Salvador. *Latin American Research Review*, 48(1), 44–67.

Hu, S., and Conrad, C. (2020). Monitoring via the courts: Judicial oversight and police violence in India. *International Studies Quarterly*, 64(3), 699–709. https://academic.oup.com/isq/article-abstract/64/3/699/5862127?redirectedFrom=fulltext.

Independent Commission of Investigations. (2020). Impact of INDECOM: Changing a culture of impunity. Government of Jamaica. https://www.indecom.gov.jm/about-us/achievements.

International Association of Chiefs of Police. (2014). *Body-Worn Cameras: Concepts and Issues Paper*. Alexandria, VA: IACP National Law Enforcement Policy Center. https://www.theiacp.org/sites/default/files/all/b/BodyWornCamerasPaper.pdf.

Inter-American Court of Human Rights. (2017). *Case of favela Nova Brasília v. Brazil. Preliminary objections, merits, reparations and costs. C, n. 333*. https://www.corteidh.or.cr/cf/Jurisprudencia2/overview.cfm?doc=1787&lang=en.

Inter-American Court of Human Rights. (2021). *Case Guerrero, Molina and Others vs. Venezuela*. https://www.corteidh.or.cr/docs/casos/articulos/seriec_424_esp.pdf.

Ivković, S.K. (2021). Presentation to the Committee on the Evidence to Advance Reform in the Global Security and Justice Sectors, National Academies of Sciences, Engineering, and Medicine, October 20, 2021. https://www.nationalacademies.org/event/08-27-2021/evidence-to-advance-reform-in-the-global-security-and-justice-sectors-workshop-3-public-session-2.

Ivković, S.K., Haberfeld, M., and Peacock, R. (2018). Decoding the code of silence. *Criminal Justice Policy Review*, 29(2), 172–189. https://doi.org/10.1177%2F0887403416680853.

Jefferson, H., Neuner, F.G., and Pasek, J. (2021). Seeing blue in black and white: Race and perceptions of officer-involved shootings. *Perspectives on Politics*, 19(4), 1165–1183. https://doi.org/10.1017/S1537592720003618.

Klockars, C.B., Ivkovich, S.K., Harver, W. E., and Haberfeld, M.R. (2000). *The Measurement of Police Integrity*. National Institute of Justice. https://www.ojp.gov/pdffiles1/nij/181465.pdf.

LaLonde, R.J. (1986). Evaluating the Econometric Evaluations of Training Programs with Experimental Data. *The American Economic Review*, 76(4), 604–620. http://www.jstor.org/stable/1806062.

Lemgruber, J. (2002). Civilian Oversight of the Police in Brazil: The case of the ombudsman's offices. Center for Studies on Public Security and Citizenship, University Candido Mendes Rio de Janeiro–Brazil.

Lemgruber, J., Cano, I., and Musumeci, L. (2017). Olho por olho?: O que pensam os cariocas sobre "bandido bom é bandido morto." *Centro de Estudos de Seguranca e Cidadania (Rio de Janeiro)*. https://www.conjur.com.br/dl/73-cariocas-acreditam-direitos-humanos.pdf.

Lemgruber, J., Musumeci, L., and Cano, I. (2003). *Quem Vigia Os Vigias? Um Estudo Sobre Controle Externo da Polícia no Brasil*. Rio de Janeiro: Record.

Lethal Force Monitor (2020). *Monitor of Use of Lethal Force in Latin America: Comparative Study of Brazil, Colombia, El Salvador, Mexico and Venezuela*. https://www.monitorfuerzaletal.com/Executive-Monitor-English.pdf.

Linos, K., and Pegram, T. (2017). What works in human rights institutions? *American Journal of International Law, 111*(3), 628–688. https://doi.org/10.1017/ajil.2017.65.

Loftin C., Wiersema B., McDowall D., Dobrin A. (2003). Underreporting of justifiable homicides committed by police officers in the United States, 1976–1998. *American Journal of Public Health, 93*(7), 1117–1121. https://doi.org/10.2105/ajph.93.7.1117.

Loyens, K. (2009). Occupational culture in policing reviewed: A comparison of values in the public and private police. *International Journal of Public Administration, 32*, 461–490. https://doi.org/10.1080/01900690902861688.

Lum, C., Stoltz, M., Koper, C.S., and Scherer, J.A. (2019). Research on body-worn cameras: What we know, what we need to know. *Criminology & Public Policy, 18*(1), 93–118. https://doi.org/10.1111/1745-9133.12412.

Lum, C., Koper, C.S., Wilson, D.B., Stoltz, M., Goodier, M., Eggins, E., Higginson, A. and Mazerolle, L. (2020). Body-worn cameras' effects on police officers and citizen behavior: A systematic review. *Campbell Systematic Reviews, 16*(3). https://doi.org/10.1002/cl2.1112.

Magaloni, B., and Rodriguez, L. (2020). Institutionalized police brutality: Torture, the militarization of security, and the reform of inquisitorial criminal justice in Mexico. *American Political Science Review, 114*(4), 1013–1034.

Marche, G. (2009). Integrity, culture, and scale: an empirical test of the big bad police agency. *Crime, Law and Social Change, 51*(5), 463–486. https://doi.org/10.1007/s10611-008-9184-7.

Miller, E.J. (2006). Role-based policing: Restraining police conduct "Outside the Legitimate Investigative Sphere." *California Law Review, 94*(3), 617–668. https://lawcat.berkeley.edu/record/1120589?ln=en.

Mitchell, R.J., Ariel, B., Firpo, M.E., Fraiman, R., del Castillo, F., Hyatt, J.M., Weinborn, C., and Brants Sabo, H. (2018). Measuring the effect of body-worn cameras on complaints in Latin America: The case of traffic police in Uruguay. *Policing: An International Journal, 41*(4), 510–524.

Muntingh, L., and Dereymaeker, G. (2013). Understanding Impunity in the South African Law Enforcement Agencies. *Civil Society Prison Reform Initiative, Community Law Centre*. https://acjr.org.za/resource-centre/understanding-impunity-in-the-south-african-law-enforcement-agencies.

National Academies of Sciences, Engineering, and Medicine (NASEM). (2018). *Proactive Policing: Effects on Crime and Communities*. Washington, DC: The National Academies Press. https://doi.org/10.17226/24928.

National Academies of Sciences, Engineering, and Medicine (NASEM). (2021). *Policing to Promote the Rule of Law and Protect the Population: An Evidence-based Approach*. Washington, DC: The National Academies Press. https://doi.org/10.17226/26217.

National Academies of Sciences, Engineering, and Medicine (NASEM). (2022). *Police Training to Promote the Rule of Law and Protect the Population*. Washington, DC: The National Academies Press. https://doi.org/10.17226/26467.

National Consensus Policy and Discussion Paper on Use of Force. (2020). National Consensus Policy and Discussion Paper on Use of Force. *International Association of Chiefs of Police*. https://www.theiacp.org/sites/default/files/2020-07/National_Consensus_Policy_On_Use_Of_Force%2007102020%20v3.pdf.

National Institute of Justice. (2009). *The Use-of-Force Continuum*. https://nij.ojp.gov/topics/articles/use-force-continuum.

National Institute of Justice. (2020). *Overview of Police Use of Force*. https://nij.ojp.gov/topics/articles/overview-police-use-force#citation--0.

Neyroud, P. (2021). *Policing "Landscapes" for the Rule of Law and Public Protection: A Review of the Available Evidence on Organizational Policies, Structures, and Human Resources.* Paper prepared for the Committee on the Evidence to Advance Reform in the Global Security and Justice Sectors, National Academies of Sciences, Engineering, and Medicine. https://www.nationalacademies.org/event/03-24-2021/evidence-to-advance-reform-in-the-global-security-and-justice-sectors-workshop-1-public-session-1.

O'Donnell, G. (2004). The quality of democracy: Why the rule of law matters. *Journal of Democracy*, 15(4), 32–46. https://www.journalofdemocracy.org/articles/the-quality-of-democracy-why-the-rule-of-law-matters/.

Osse, A., and Cano, I. (2017). Police deadly use of firearms: An international comparison. *The International Journal of Human Rights*, 27(5), 629–649. https://doi.org/10.1080/13642987.2017.1307828.

Owens, E., Weisburd, D., Amendola, K.L., and Alpert, G.P. (2018). Can you build a better cop? Experimental evidence on supervision, training, and policing in the community. *Criminology & Public Policy*, 17, 41–87. https://doi.org/10.1111/1745-9133.12337.

Panel of Experts on Policing and Crowd Management (2018). *Final Report*, 27 May, 2018. http://www.policesecretariat.gov.za/downloads/Panel_Experts_Report.pdf.

Paoline, E.A., and Terrill, W. (2007). Police education, experience, and the use of force. *Criminal Justice and Behavior*, 34, 179–195. https://doi.org/10.1177/0093854806290239.

Papachristos, A.V. (2015). Use of data can stop crime by helping potential victims. *The New York Times*. Nov 18, 2015.

Peeples, L. (2020). What the data say about police brutality and racial bias—and which reforms might work. *Nature*, 583, 22–24. https://www.nature.com/articles/d41586-020-01846-z.

Pelfrey Jr., W.V, and Keener, S. (2016). Police body worn cameras: A mixed method approach assessing perceptions of efficacy. *Policing: An International Journal*, 39(3), 491–506. https://doi.org/10.1108/PIJPSM-02-2016-0019.

President's Task Force on 21st Century Policing. (2015). *The President's Task Force on 21st Century Policing Implementation Guide: Moving from Recommendations to Action*. Washington, DC: Office of Community Oriented Policing Service. https://cops.usdoj.gov/RIC/Publications/cops-p341-pub.pdf.

Probert, T. (2018). *Police Attitudes and Crowd Management in Africa: Exploring the Impact of Soft-Law Instruments and Training in Malawi*. Mowbray: The Danish Institute for Human Rights. http://apcof.org/wp-content/uploads/police-attitudes-and-crowd-management-in-africa-exploring-the-impact-of-soft-law-instruments-and-training-in-malawi-thomas-probert.pdf.

Rajah, V.K. (2012). Panel discussion: Measuring the rule of law. *Singapore Journal of Legal Studies*, 331–356. http://www.jstor.org/stable/24872215.

Resnick, B. (2020). Police brutality is a public health crisis. *Vox* https://www.vox.com/science-and-health/2020/6/1/21276828/pandemic-protests-police-public-health-black-lives-matter.

Rosa, F.G., and Cano, I. (2016). Letal dade policial no Rio de Janeiro: Fatores de influência individual e medidas de controle institucional. *Projeto Segurança Cidadã*. https://dspace.mj.gov.br/handle/1/3419.

Rushin, S. (2014). Federal enforcement of police reform. *Fordham Law Review*, 82(6). https://ir.lawnet.fordham.edu/flr/vol82/iss6/20.

Rushin, S. (2015). Structural reform litigation in American police departments. *Minnesota Law Review*, 99, 1343–1422. https://www.minnesotalawreview.org/wp-content/uploads/2019/07/Rushin_pdf1.pdf.

Shane, J.M. (2018). Improving Police Use of Force: A Policy Essay on National Data Collection. *Criminal Justice Policy Review*, 29(2), 128–148.

Shields R.T., and Ward, B.W. (2008). Comparison of the National Violent Death Reporting System and Supplementary Homicide Report: Potential benefits of integration. *Justice Research and Policy*, 10(2), 67–97. https://www.ojp.gov/ncjrs/virtual-library/abstracts/comparison-national-violent-death-reporting-system-and.

Smith, N.R. (2019). *Contradictions of Democracy: Vigilantism and Rights in Post-Apartheid South Africa*. Oxford University Press.

Sousa, W., Miethe, T., and Sakiyama, M. (2018). Inconsistencies in public opinion of body-worn cameras on police: Transparency, trust, and improved police–citizen relationships. *Policing (Oxford)*, 12, 100–108. https://doi.org/10.1093/police/pax015.

Stott, C., Ho, L., Radburn, M., Chan, Y.T., Kyprianides, A., and Morales, P.S. (2021). Patterns of "disorder" during the 2019 protests in Hong Kong: Policing, social identity, intergroup dynamics, and radicalization. *Policing: A Journal of Policy and Practice*, 14(4), 814–835. https://doi.org/10.1093/police/paaa073.

Tait, S. (2021). *Use of Force Policies and Fundamental International Human Rights Law*. Presentation to the Committee on the Evidence to Advance Reform in the Global Security and Justice Sectors, National Academies of Sciences, Engineering, and Medicine, October 22, 2021. https://www.nationalacademies.org/event/08-27-2021/evidence-to-advance-reform-in-the-global-security-and-justice-sectors-workshop-3-public-session-2.

Tate, J., Jenkins, J., and Rich, S. (2022). Police shootings database 2015–2022. *The Washington Post*. https://www.washingtonpost.com/graphics/investigations/police-shootings-database/.

Tennenbaum, A.N. (1994). The Influence of the Garner Decision on Police Use of Deadly Force. *Journal of Criminal Law and Criminology*, 85(1), 241–260. https://scholarlycommons.law.northwestern.edu/cgi/viewcontent.cgi?article=6811&context=jclc.

Transparency International (2018). Whistleblower Protection in the European Union - Analysis of and Recommendations to the Proposed EU Directive. Berlin: Transparency International. https://www.transparency.org/en/publications/whistleblower-protection-in-the-eu-analysis-of-and-recommendations.

Tusalem, R.F. (2019). Examining the determinants of extra-judicial killings in the Philippines at the subnational level: The role of penal populism and vertical accountability. *Human Rights Review*, 20, 67–101. https://doi.org/10.1007/s12142-018-0535-1.

United Nations. (1979). *Code of Conduct for Law Enforcement Officials*. General Assembly resolution, 34–169. Office of the Commissioner for Human Rights. https://www.ohchr.org/en/professionalinterest/pages/lawenforcementofficials.aspx.

United Nations. (2009). *Human Rights Standards in the Use of Force*. UN Peacekeeping PDT Standards, Specialized Training Material for Police (1st Ed.).

United Nations Committee Against Torture. (2006). Communication no 273/2005. http://digitallibrary.un.org/record/576962/files/CAT_C_36_D_273_2005_Rev.1-FR.pdf.

United Nations Human Rights Council. (2020). *Universal Periodic Review*. https://www.ohchr.org/en/hrbodies/upr/pages/uprmain.aspx.

United Nations High Commissioner for Human Rights. (1997). *International Human Rights Standards for Law Enforcement: A Pocket Book on Human Rights for the Police*. https://www.un.org/ruleoflaw/files/training5Add1en.pdf.

United Nations Human Rights Council. (2021). *OHCHR Report on Promotion and Protection of the Human Rights and Fundamental Freedoms of Africans and of People of African Descent Against Excessive Use of Force and Other Human Rights Violations by Law Enforcement Officers* (A/HRC/47/53). 47th session of the Human Rights Council. https://www.ohchr.org/en/NewsEvents/Pages/DisplayNews.aspx?NewsID=27296&LangID=E.

United States Commission on Civil Rights. (2018). *Police Use of Force: An Examination of Modern Policing Practices*. United States Commission on Civil Rights. https://www.usccr.gov/files/pubs/2018/11-15-Police-Force.pdf.

United States Department of State. (2016). *INL Guide to Police Assistance*. U.S. Department of State's Bureau of International Narcotics and Law Enforcement Affairs (INL), Office of Criminal Justice Assistance and Partnership.

Van Ness, L. (2020). Body cameras may not be the easy answer everyone was looking for. PEW Charitable Trusts. https://www.pewtrusts.org/en/research-and-analysis/blogs/stateline/2020/01/14/body-cameras-may-not-be-the-easy-answer-everyone-was-looking-for.

Versteeg, M., and Ginsburg, T. (2017). Measuring the Rule of Law: A Comparison of Indicators. *Law & Social Inquiry*, 42(1), 100–137. https://doi.org/10.1111/lsi.12175.

Weisburd, D., Telep, C.W., Vovak, H., Zastrow, T., Braga, A.A., and Turchan, B. (2022). Reforming the police through procedural justice training: A multicity randomized trial at crime hot spots. *The Proceedings of the National Academy of Sciences*, 119(4), e2118780119. https://doi.org/10.1073/pnas.2118780119.

White, M.D., and Orosco, C. (2021). *Testing the Impact of De-escalation Training on Officer Behavior: The Tempe (AZ) Smart Policing Initiative*. Arizona State University Center for Violence Prevention and Community Safety. https://www.smart-policing.com/sites/default/files/inline-files/Tempe%20SPI%20Final%20Report%2012-21.pdf.

Wolfe, S.E., and Piquero, A.R. (2011). Organizational justice and police misconduct. *Criminal Justice and Behavior*, 38(4), 332–353. https://doi.org/10.1177/0093854810397739.

Wood, T. (1997). *Royal Commission into the New South Wales Police Service, Final Report Volume I: Corruption*. Sydney: The Government of the State of New South Wales. https://www.australianpolice.com.au/wp-content/uploads/2017/05/RCPS-Report-Volume-1.pdf.

Wood, G., Tyler, T.R., and Papachristos, A.V. (2020). Procedural justice training reduces police use of force and complaints against officers. *Proceedings of the National Academy of Sciences of the United States of America*, 117, 9815–9821. https://doi.org/10.1073/pnas.1920671117.

Zimring, F.E. (2017). *When Police Kill*. Cambridge, MA: Harvard University Press.

Zoorob, M. (2020). Do Police Brutality Stories Reduce 911 Calls? Reassessing an Important Criminological Finding. *American Sociological Review*, 85(1), 176–183. https://doi.org/10.1177%2F0003122419895254.

Appendix

Biographical Sketches of Committee Members and Staff

Lawrence W. Sherman (*Chair*) is the Wolfson professor of criminology emeritus and director of the Police Executive Programme at the University of Cambridge Institute of Criminology. He previously served as head of the criminology departments at Cambridge, University of Pennsylvania, and University of Maryland, and as president of the American Society of Criminology, the American Academy of Political and Social Science, and the Academy of Experimental Criminology. He has designed or led over 50 randomized field experiments in police agencies on three continents, which formed the basis for his leadership of the global professional movement for evidence-based policing, notably through the U.K. Society for Evidence-Based Policing and its counterparts in Australia, New Zealand, the United States, and Canada. As one of six authors of the report to the U.S. Congress on *Preventing Crime: What Works, What Doesn't, What's Promising*, he wrote the chapter on the Maryland Scientific Methods Scale for rank-ordering the strength of evidence from impact evaluations, which has been adapted by a number of governments for their "what works" agendas on crime prevention. He has edited two volumes of the *ANNALS of the American Academy of Political and Social Science* on police and violence, most recently on reducing fatal police shootings. Sherman earned his Ph.D. in sociology from Yale University.

Beatriz Abizanda is a senior specialist in the citizen security cluster of the Inter-American Development Bank (IDB). Her professional experience spans the private and public sectors in Latin America and Europe. She has led the design, implementation, and technical advisory of major IDB criminal justice reform projects in the citizen security sector. Her projects include police modernization, prison reform, and youth violence prevention components for programs in Belize, Brazil, Colombia, Costa Rica, Ecuador, and Uruguay. She has also co-authored the IDB's conceptual framework and operational guidelines for citizen security and coexistence and contributed to the World Bank's World Development Report. She is currently conducting meta-analytic research on the effectiveness of interventions for domestic violence perpetrators. She is a member of the jury of the Stockholm Prize in criminology and is on the editorial board of the *Journal of International Criminology*. Abizanda received a M.A. in criminology from the University of Cambridge and an MBA from Georgetown University.

Abigail Allen is an associate program officer with the National Academies of Sciences, Engineering, and Medicine's Committee on Law and Justice. Previously, she worked during law school as a criminal defense law clerk, and as a legislative affairs intern and legal researcher with the Animal Legal Defense Fund. Her research and writing were centered on projects related to COVID-19's impact on the factory farming industry and aquatic animal law issues. Allen received her B.A. in criminology, law, and society and a J.D. from George Mason University.

Emily Backes is associate director of the Committee on Law and Justice in the Division of Behavioral and Social Sciences and Education at the National Academies of Sciences, Engineering, and Medicine. She has served as the study director for the reports *The Promise of Adolescence: Realizing Opportunity for All Youth* and *Transforming the Financing of Early Care and Education*. In her time at the Academies, she has directed studies and provided analytical and editorial assistance to projects covering a range of topics, including juvenile justice, policing, forensic science, illicit markets, science literacy, science communication, and human rights. Backes received an M.A. and B.A. in history from the University of Missouri, specializing in U.S. human rights policy and international law. She also received a J.D. from the University of the District of Columbia, where she represented clients as a student attorney with the Low-income Taxpayer Clinic and the Juvenile and Special Education Law Clinic.

Yanilda María González is an assistant professor of public policy at the Harvard Kennedy School. Her research focuses on policing, state violence, and citizenship in democracy, examining how race, class, and other forms of inequality shape these processes. Her book *Authoritarian Police in Democracy: Contested Security in Latin America* studies the persistence of police forces as authoritarian enclaves in otherwise democratic states, demonstrating how ordinary democratic politics in unequal societies can both reproduce authoritarian policing and bring about rare moments of expansive reforms. Previously, she was an assistant professor at the School of Social Service Administration at the University of Chicago and has worked at a number of human rights organizations in the United States and Argentina, including the New York Civil Liberties Union, and Equipo Latino Américano de Justicia y Género. González received her Ph.D. in politics and social policy from Princeton University.

Guy Grossman is professor of political science at the University of Pennsylvania. His research is in applied political economy, with substantive focus on governance, migration, security, and conflict processes. He is founder and co-director of the University of Pennsylvania's Development Research Initiative, a member of the Evidence in Governance and Politics network, faculty affiliate of Stanford's Immigration Policy Lab, and the University of Pennsylvania's Identity & Conflict Lab. He designed and carried out field studies in a large number of developing countries, in collaboration with various international agencies, including the World Bank, the U.K. Department for International Development, the U.S. Agency for International Development, as well as with African governments and local non-governmental organizations. His work has appeared in the *Proceedings of the National Academy of Sciences*, *the American Political Science Review*, *American Journal of Political Science*, *International Organization*, and *Journal of Politics*, among other journals. Grossman received his M.A. in political philosophy and LL.B. in law from Tel-Aviv University and a Ph.D. in political science from Columbia University.

John L. Hagan is the John D. MacArthur professor of sociology and law at Northwestern University, and his primary areas of expertise are in criminology, criminal justice, and international criminal law. He is a member of the National Academy of Sciences and fellow of the American Academy of Arts and Sciences and the Royal Society of Canada. He is best known with co-author Alberto Palloni for their mortality estimate of the Darfur genocide published in *Science* and his book co-authored with Wenona Rymond-Richmond on *Darfur and the Crime of Genocide*. He is also the author of *Who Are the Criminals? The Politics of Crime Policy from the Age of Roosevelt to the Age of Reagan* and with Bill McCarthy, *Mean Streets: Youth Crime and Homelessness*. He has received the John Simon Guggenheim Foundation Fellowship, the Stockholm Prize in criminology, the Harry Kalven Prize from the Law & Society Association, and the Cesare Beccaria Gold Medal from the German Society of Criminology. Hagan received his M.A. and Ph.D in sociology from the University of Alberta.

Karen Hall is deputy executive director at the Rule of Law Collaborative. Previously, she was associate professor and director of the master of law program in democratic governance and rule of law at the Ohio Northern University Pettit College of Law. She also served with the U.S. Department of State in its Bureau of International Narcotics and Law Enforcement Affairs. While there, she directed the development and management of assistance to the criminal justice system in Afghanistan as part of the overall U.S. foreign assistance initiative. She has also developed programs dealing with institutional reform, access to justice, protection of women's rights, and legal education. She has lived at the U.S. Embassy in Kabul, Afghanistan, where she directly managed the State Department's criminal justice and corrections programs. In recognition of her work, she earned multiple meritorious and superior honor awards from the State Department. Her teaching interests include international rule of law reform, international law, comparative criminal law, rule of law program design and management, student externship courses, and introduction to the American legal system. Her current research involves examining the consequences of the appropriations and administrative processes of the U.S. government in relation to rule of law reform worldwide. Hall received an M.A. in security studies from Georgetown School of Foreign Service and her J.D. from Harvard Law School.

Cynthia Lum is a professor of criminology, law, and society, and the director of the Center for Evidence-Based Crime Policy at George Mason University. She is a leading authority on evidence-based policing—an approach to policing reform advocating that research, evaluation, analysis, and scientific processes have "a seat at the table" in law enforcement policy making and practice. Her research focuses on improving law enforcement patrol and investigative operations through rigorous field research and evaluations. She has also developed numerous tools and strategies to translate and institutionalize research into everyday law enforcement activities. She is the author of *Evidence-Based Policing: Translating Research into Practice*, one of the leading volumes on the subject. She has trained thousands of police officers in the United States and around the world on evidence-based policing strategies and approaches, including for the State Department's International Law Enforcement Academy. Lum received a Ph.D. in criminology and criminal justice from the University of Maryland, College Park.

Emily Owens is a professor of criminology, law, and society as well as economics at the University of California, Irvine. She studies a wide range of topics in the economics of crime, including policing, sentencing, and the impact of local public policies on criminal behavior. Her research examines how government policies affect the prevalence of criminal activity as well as how agents within the criminal justice system, particularly police, prosecutors, and judges, respond to policy changes. She is engaged in ongoing research projects on police training, alcohol regulation, immigration policy, and local economic development programs. Owens received her Ph.D. in economics from the University of Maryland, College Park.

Sarah Perumattam is a senior program assistant with the National Academies of Sciences, Engineering, and Medicine's Committee on Law and Justice and Board on Children, Youth, and Families. Her undergraduate research focused on disaster relief and humanitarian response, culminating in her senior capstone project, *Improving HIV/AIDS Treatment in Humanitarian Response: Lessons Learned from Rwanda*. She served as an international teaching assistants' consultant at Brown's Center for Language Studies and studied abroad in Seoul, South Korea, where she worked as a guest editor for the Yonsei University Annals. Perumattam graduated from Brown University with a bachelor's degree in public policy and a specialization in government, law, and ethics.

Julie Anne Schuck (*Study Director*) is a senior program officer at the National Academies of Sciences, Engineering, and Medicine. She has provided analytical, administrative, and editorial support for many studies and workshops and served as a technical writer for many reports. Her projects have covered a wide range of subjects, including law and justice issues; national security; STEM (science, technology, engineering, and mathematic) education; the science of human-system integration, workforce development, and the evaluations of several federal research programs. Notably, she was part of the staff team that supported the committee that produced the report *The Growth of Incarceration in the United States: Exploring Causes and Consequences*. Schuck has a B.S. in engineering physics from the University of California, San Diego, and an M.S. in education from Cornell University.

Justice Tankebe is a lecturer in criminology and a fellow at St. Edmund's College, University of Cambridge. Prior to his current appointment, he was a teaching associate on the Police Executive Programme at the Institute of Criminology, Cambridge. His research interests lie in policing, legitimation and legitimacy, organisational justice, corruption, vigilantism and extralegal punishment, comparative criminology, sociology of law, and crime and criminal justice in sub-Saharan Africa. Tankebe's current research projects include legitimacy and counter-terrorism policing, corruption among prospective elites, sentencing decision-making in Ghana, the death penalty in Africa, and police self-legitimacy. Tankebe received a Ph.D. in criminology from the University of Cambridge.

Sunia Young is a senior program assistant with the National Academies of Sciences, Engineering, and Medicine's Committee on Law and Justice and Board on Children, Youth, and Families. She previously worked as a case manager at a Washington, DC-based behavioral health organization. Young also interned at the Carter Center's Mental Health Program and with a DC-based organization that supports Asian women who have experienced domestic violence and sexual assault. Additionally, she has studied the Persian language extensively and spent the summer of 2018 in Tajikistan studying the Iranian and Tajik dialects of Persian through the United States Department of State. Young graduated from Davidson College with a bachelor's degree in psychology and a minor in Arab studies.